CW01626537

Life's a Gamble

Leena Takooree

All rights reserved © Madeleena Takooree 2023

The right of Madeleena Takooree to be identified as the Author of this work has been asserted by her in accordance with the Copyright, Designs and Patent Act 1988.

No part of this publication may be reproduced, distributed, or transmitted, in any form or by any means, electronic, mechanical, photocopying, recording, or otherwise, without first obtaining the written permission of the rights owner, except for the use of brief quotations in reviews.

Editing & Proofreading: Christine Irwin, Rosie Garrard & Sandee Knight Sond
Cover Design: Ben Errington
Cover Photographer: Aleksandra Modzelewska

ISBN: 978-1-3999-5130-2

For my friend Alexandra Peart
May 1st 1990 – May 3rd 2012

CONTENTS

ACKNOWLEDGEMENTS

Writing and completing this book would have been impossible without the support of my friends and family over the years. Christine, Rosie, and Sandee this book would not have existed without you, thank you.
A huge shout out to my friend Ben for bringing the design of my book cover to life, thanks for designing exactly what I had in mind and for your patience throughout.

INTRO

Hey! Welcome to my book, my name is Leena and I hope what you read here helps you, helps someone else or is just a good read; I hope it is anyway as it sure was one hell of a journey.
If you are reading this, then thank you so much for picking me up! I hope that this book helps you through a tough time if you are going through something like what I went through in 2006. I want you to know that you are not alone; even if it feels like you are.
To those of you who don't know me I hope after reading this book you will know me just that little bit more. To those of you that are close to me, I hope this story brings us closer together and that you can know perhaps just that little bit more detail, the things that I maybe hide away or don’t talk about.

Where do we begin?

In 2006, at the age of eighteen I was diagnosed with Acute Myeloid Leukaemia (AML).

Yup, the big C. Cancer.

My final round of chemo was followed by pneumonia and then suffering from a stroke. I started writing this book about 11 (yes ELEVEN) years ago, however it became harder and harder to write and I found it too hard to go over the past, so I just left it on my PC untouched perhaps to come back to it at a later date, so here we are. I mean, I often thought about picking it back up again and writing, I had a notepad next to my bed where I would jot things down that I wanted to add to the book, so as much as this book could have been finished all those years ago, I am actually pleased that I am only just finishing it now because I have had that time to recover, heal and now I am able to give you a better view of my story, of my life.

A lot of what I wrote 11 years ago seemed disjointed or just didn't seem "right" or "good enough". Good enough for me, that is, not the reader. In the past few months, I've been thinking about my story and remembering how much I have overcome but also realised that maybe talking about it may help someone else, it may help you. I find it helps even now to talk about it, because after overcoming something so huge in my life, with the daily struggles that I still encounter since the stroke, talking just makes things easier.

I bottled stuff up for such a long time in the start because I was scared to be viewed differently or to be judged.

The thing is we are all different and we will all be judged whether it be by someone else, or by ourselves and I'm okay with that. So, if by writing this just helps me, then great...if it helps you then even better - that would make my day.

Now I'm not saying *oh hey look at me I'm the kid that had cancer* (I'm now 35, but I'm still a kid at heart…) what I am saying is, you are not alone.

When I was going through all the treatment at the age of 18 in 2006, I would have loved to have been reading someone else's story.

To know I wasn't alone would have meant the absolute world. I of course was never alone, I have the best family and friends in the world, who never left my side and I will be forever grateful, but to have someone to relate to that knows what it's like to throw up after swallowing a piece of food because it's a side effect to chemo, or to wake up each morning to be faced with even more hair falling off your head and seeing it stuck to your pillow...or to be so weak that you physically can't stand or function that you have to have your Mum brush your teeth, it just would have been good to have someone that I could relate to, someone that knew what I was going through.

Amongst all the company I had, often it felt like the loneliest place in the world. This isn't anything anyone did wrong, it was just a very lonely place because everyone around you says all the right things and does the right things, but they are helpless, you are helpless. This feeling does pass, it is just something I often battled with and learning to get myself out of that took some time.

One thing I learnt. Hope. There is always hope...I say there's one thing I learnt: I'm lying. There are so many things I have learnt and continue to learn after going through the worst time of my life.

I mean this from the bottom of my heart - please reach out and ask me anything if it can help you, let me help you. I will make the time for you, even if I do not know you. It won't be an easy journey and no two stories are the same - but that's the best thing. Share your story, be heard.

Does it scare me to put so much of me out there for everyone to see? No, I've been more scared of other things in life. What scares me is that someone out there might be struggling and that's not okay. If you know someone going through any form of treatment however big or small it is to you, to them it may seem like the end of the world. Make their day, send them a message, they might not be up to replying but it doesn't mean they are ignoring you, without a doubt they are probably pleased that they aren't forgotten.

The 'Cancer World' is its own little bubble. Depending on

the type of cancer you have, or the treatment needed it can range from feeling "normal" to feeling like absolute crap within hours. Keep fighting, you will smile again. You may have the most incredible journey and escape all the side effects and I hope that you do! There were times where I thought *this isn't too bad?* and those good days were the days that I smiled, even if the next day was absolute hell there are good moments within the bad.

This book may appear disjointed or in sections please bear with me – there is roughly ten months in hospital to cover and the five years plus after that which was spent going to numerous appointments.

You are now on the journey of my life. Grab a cuppa and some chocolate, settle in, and enjoy.

CHAPTER 1

WHERE IT ALL BEGAN

Around the start of May 2006, I noticed loads of bruising on my body. They seemed weird; they all stayed in an almost yellow-ish state and never seemed to heal. They just kept appearing on my body. I was a drummer in a band at the time, our band was called Incured. I just assumed that the bruising was from moving the drumkit around, playing gigs or from going to gigs - I liked going into mosh pits at the time. I wouldn't recommend them at all, you'll now catch me trying to run away from them.

I ignored the bruising for a few days, maybe it was even a week; but then, one weekend that same month, I became out of breath just walking a few steps. I also lost a lot (I mean a LOT) of blood from well...downstairs shall we say. Which was not normal in the slightest, it wasn't my "time of the month."

Alongside these symptoms I also felt super dizzy anytime I moved, I couldn't concentrate due to feeling so exhausted, I didn't feel my normal so called "hyper" self.

I mentioned the bruising and the bleeding to my Mum, and she said I should go to the doctor to get checked out. As it was a weekend, we had to wait until they opened on Monday. The thought of seeing a doctor sounded scary, but I thought they must have something to stop me feeling so drained and explain all the bruises that kept on appearing but never healing. Fast forward to Monday; waiting rooms suck. The smell, the sick people...I really dislike them. We were called in quickly by the GP, even though it felt like forever. The doctor looked at my bruising, listened to my other symptoms and said perhaps it was an iron deficiency. My Mum was adamant for me to have a blood test and that we wouldn't leave until it was done. I am insanely grateful that my Mum stood her ground and made sure I had that blood test done, even after I said, "Mum they don't have any appointments, it's fine". The doctor luckily found one slot.

Mum, if you are reading this - thank you for making sure they took my blood on that day, I love you forever.

Back to the waiting room we went. The nurse called my name "Madeleena?" (Yeah, Leena is my nickname by the way). We went to the little room where the lovely nurse popped a needle into my arm to draw out the required blood needed for the vials. Once the needle was out...my arm wouldn't stop bleeding. I say this lightly, but the blood was pouring down my arm, it looked like something out of a horror movie. The nurse's reaction made me feel uneasy, she looked worried and had the *'there's definitely something wrong here'* look on her face. The bleeding eventually stopped...twenty minutes later.
Now I don't recall ever having my blood taken before this day, but I'm pretty sure I had lost enough blood at that point. I'm also pretty sure that, after applying a little pressure, blood shouldn't freak out like that. I was tired and zoned out, but that scared me. I thought jeez, lack of iron you say. GIVE ME THE IRON TABLETS. They said they would let us know the results later if there were any problems or issues that might be of concern, but if we don't hear from them; then no news is good news.

After the blood test, my parents dropped me to college. They said they would pick me up after as I was still so exhausted that the idea of getting the two busses home was not something I wanted to do. I walked a few steps before seeing some of my friends and my then boyfriend in their car listening to music, I was a bit early for my next lesson, so I joined them. Roll on 5 minutes later and I was physically too tired to even walk the short journey from the car park to the college. I could just about stand up. I called my parents, who turned back around to pick me up. I mean, we have all felt drained and tired, but I had never felt so unwell, so weak or THIS tired before. I knew I was unfit, but this just didn't seem right. I thought after some sleep I'd feel better - I think I pretty much slept through the rest of the day.
I remember being on the phone later that evening to my boyfriend at the time who I won't name, because this is my story, not his. However, he and his family were the greatest support during the crap time I went through, and we went on to be together for 8 years.

(For the purpose of this story, we will name him BFATT - boyfriend at the time. Thanks for the suggestion, Sandee - I love it.)

I remember it being around 9:30pm, I said to BFATT that I needed to get off the phone so I could try and get some more sleep, when I heard a loud knock at the door. We don't usually get anyone coming to the house past 6pm and if we do it is usually my sister who has a key and no need to knock. Then I heard an unfamiliar voice say my name, "Madeleena", which no one ever called or calls me. Next thing I know my Mum has walked into my room and said I need to go downstairs. I put the phone down and plodded downstairs in my pyjamas to see why I needed to leave my warm bed. There was a man in the front room, he had a lanyard around his neck, curly hair and maybe glasses on...however I didn't have

my own glasses on so everything else was just a literal blur. He seemed anxious, anxious to tell someone something, but I wasn't sure who or what. He had a file on his lap, Mum looked concerned and all this time I was sat there thinking why have I been dragged out of bed to be ignored? I think my Dad and brother were in the garage at the time, doing something car related as usual. It turned out that this guy was there to see me, he was the on-call doctor who had been given my results and was sent to tell me that I needed to urgently go to hospital. I assume he had left in such a rush to get to my house that he didn't check the file and expected to be breaking the news to someone older than me.
He for some reason thought that "Madeleena Takooree" was perhaps someone more elderly, not an eighteen-year-old. As soon as he realised, he quickly apologised and explained my results had come back and that I needed to go to the Oncology here in Bristol immediately.
I asked what was wrong but to this day everything he said is a blur, I don't remember changing out of my pyjamas, but I do remember my parents driving us to the hospital and me being tired and confused.
I remember my Dad driving to the hospital and parking in the dark, dimly lit car park. I then remember taking my time to want to get out of the car because I just had a bad feeling, the building looked scary, and it had a heavy feeling on me when I looked at it. As I got out of the car and closed the door behind me, I slowly started walking up towards the hospital doors. I remember thinking *this isn't right?* I want to go home. I want to go home.
That moment will forever be embedded in my mind. I think we got there around 11pm-midnight, we had to ring the buzzer to be let in. We were told that the visiting hours had passed, my parents then stated my name and the reaction was "she's here!"
I was really freaked out as the doors opened, two nurses approached me, and they led me and my parents down a

dimly lit hospital corridor to a side room.

Ward 62, Room 4.

CHAPTER 2

CANCER

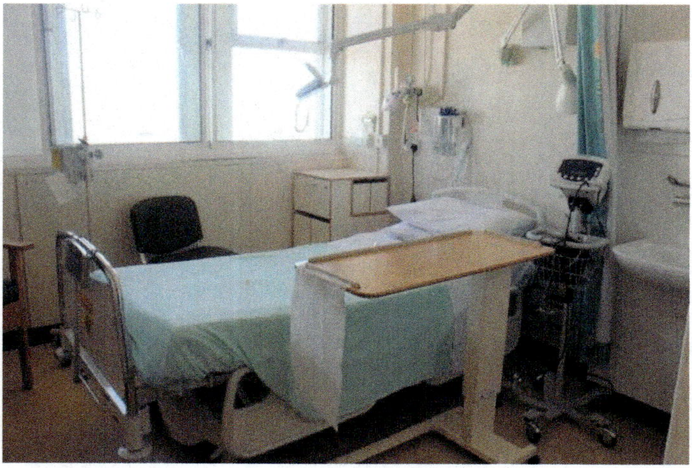

In 2011, I did a Foundation Degree in Photography, I used imagery based around the time I had cancer for my final exhibition. This is the very room I was in when they told me I had cancer. I took this photo 5 years after being diagnosed, walking back into this room was physically and emotionally hard. It smelt the same and it looked like the day I walked in and had my whole life change drastically in a few moments. Let's go back to the 8th of May 2006. From midnight until

the early hours of the morning, I was having numerous tests, talking to several doctors and nurses, and having my blood pressure taken.
This is all such a blur looking back, I remember at the time feeling so confused as to why I was in that room and what the hell was going on. I soon discovered that the machine in the image on the right-hand side of the bed was soon to become something I would see every single morning.
That machine was the least of my worries. I called it an 'obs' machine as I heard a nurse refer to it as that once. It takes your blood pressure, monitors your heart rate and in the little shelf underneath it, sat an in-ear thermometer - I had to have my temperature taken daily.
I wish I could remember everything said to me and the timescale of things over the early morning hours, but I just remember feeling lost. I remember thinking my parents looked upset and scared, I had never seen them look like that before. I wondered if they had worked out why I was in here, or maybe they took in everything that was being said to me. In that moment, I think everyone knew how bad things were, everyone but me. I was ready to go home. This suddenly seemed a lot more serious than an iron deficiency.

My Mum stayed with me that night, neither of us slept.

The next morning, I had a Groshong line put in. A Groshong line is an intravenous catheter, which can be left in place for long periods of time. For example, when you need to have chemotherapy. The line went into a vein on my chest, it was a very strange feeling to look down and see that embedded in your body. I still have the scars from where the Groshong line was. I am glad I have these scars on my body, as it is a little reminder of what I have been through. No scar that has been left on me mounts up to how it felt to go through what I call, my experience of hell. Mum called Dad in the morning around 9am to let him know we were up and to come back to the hospital when he was ready, he was there within 20 minutes. I could tell he hadn't had any sleep either. That day was a big day, as from the blood samples that they had taken over the early hours of the morning they could tell us all what was wrong. I didn't know what to expect, or again, what was going on. This day in my head is still a little bit unclear and disjointed. I was told the news before my friends came to visit; however, I am unsure on the timings of being told. I just hoped I was going to be told this was all a mistake and that I could go home.

Unfortunately, this was not the case.

Later that day, BFATT and my friends Sandee, Laura, Sophie, Becky, and Izzy came to the hospital to see me.
My consultant came into my room, everyone went outside, except my Mum and Dad; it was that moment I was told I had been diagnosed with Acute Myeloid Leukaemia (AML). Trying to be strong I didn't cry. Or more so, I don't think I quite understood, or wanted to understand what those three words meant. Dr Evely (my consultant) talked me through what this all meant. He said numerous things would happen, and that treatment needed to start immediately. He discussed things such as having to undergo chemotherapy treatment, daily blood tests, how many courses of treatment there might be and many other side effects. All I remember hearing loudly amongst the whole list of chaos was "your hair will fall out". In all honesty hearing that I would lose my hair was the part that hit me the most; I guess what was happening to me finally hit.
I remember thinking *hang on? I'm that sick? Like the people on the TV, and the stories you hear on the news about other people? Other people get ill, not me. That's what I have...CANCER?*

Cancer. Cancer. Cancer.

I didn't really understand all the talk about white cells, red cells, and platelets at the time so all that was going through one ear and out of the other. I know it might seem vain to only cry when finding out that I would lose my hair, but this is the one thing I associated with all those people on TV that were ill, they were bald. They were so ill that something for some reason caused their hair to fall out, what on earth could that be. Well, I was soon going to find out. Great. I didn't think the treatment would be too hard, or too long. I was wrong. My Mum burst into tears and couldn't stop. My Dad tried to tell my Mum to stop and not to cry in front of me and that they had to be strong for me, but even I could see the tears in my Dad's eyes. After I was told my diagnosis Dr Evely asked me if I wanted to tell my friends or if I preferred him to break the bad news. I asked him to tell my friends for me, as I could not stop crying and couldn't really handle any of it myself. He went out of the room to talk to my friends in the next room. I could hear their reactions through the wall, which made me cry even more.

CANCER.

Are you sure? Have they double checked? Were they my blood samples? Maybe they got mixed up? Then I realised, they took so many samples of blood and ran SO many tests that it wasn't a mistake. As much as I wanted it to be, it couldn't be.

Yeah. Cancer.

I remember Sandee coming back into the room first in a flood of tears, she hugged me and the first thing I said was "I don't want to lose my hair". She was then shortly followed by my other friends Sophie, Becky, Laura, and Izzy. All of them were crying, it hurt so much to see that. BFATT came in next, he walked towards me and held my hand so tightly. For me this was one of the worst moments and believe me there were many more to come. Being in a room and seeing all my friends and family crying. The only thing that was running through my mind at the time was '*be strong, stop crying and make them smile*', for once I couldn't. It broke my heart to see them all cry; it broke my heart. I realised that having a tube in my chest and knowing that all my hair was going to fall out was probably not going to be the worst thing I would come across. That feeling of hearing the word 'Cancer' will always suck. To be told that it was something I had, was every single emotion you could imagine times a trillion. I will say this – I am crying whilst writing this part of my book, because even though it was 17 years ago, to go over this all and to relive it, is so hard. It is something I will never forget, and I never want to forget. Now, don't get me wrong everyone will have their own story, your journey may be an absolute breeze, but mine wasn't. There were days where I felt like I was fine, then an hour later I'd be throwing up and feeling absolutely rubbish.

Go with the feeling, you just have to tackle one day at a time. This is how I have lived my life since then, no one can tell you how you might feel or react to something, but if you are surrounded by friends and family, I promise you they make this so much easier even when you are at your lowest.

Wednesday 10th May 2006, first stage of chemo:

This treatment was for 10 days, I had to take around 10-16 tablets a day. I have never liked tablets; these became more and more difficult to take over my first course of chemo. I vividly remember one time it took me over an hour a half to take them. Then I threw up and had to take a fresh batch all over again. It wasn't pleasant.

One of many side effects of the treatment were ulcers in my mouth. This made it even more difficult to take the tablets. The first stage seemed long and endless; I didn't like being in the hospital bed at all. My Mum stayed in my room with me in the week, BFATT usually stayed on the weekends to give my Mum a break. Whoever stayed with me slept in a reclining chair. If you have ever been to a hospital, those chairs that you see in the outpatient's day unit, that is what they slept in. I couldn't imagine how uncomfortable it must've been to sleep in, but they did it anyway. They did it for me.

It wasn't long until I lost my appetite, soon I was sleeping all the time too. By sleep I mean I was just wiped out from all the drugs. The side effects varied as to how they made me feel, some were worse than others. I hated that the smell of food made me feel nauseous. I love food, you'd be mad not to and let me tell you there is nothing better than your Mum's cooking after eating hospital food. You learn to appreciate so much in life after going through something like this, even the small things like your Mum's cooking; don't take it for granted. The food wasn't as bad as I thought it would be, some days had better food than other days, and it all depended on day by day as to how I would feel. When the food came into the room, they would uncover it and the smell of the food would often make me want to throw up. It wasn't that it smelt bad, it was just one of MANY side effects. All the side effects were bad, every single one. They made me feel like complete rubbish, the treatment drains the life out of you too. I tried my best to put a smile on my face and to not be put down by all of this, even though I hated it. I won't lie but it was tough, and this was just the first course of chemo, I still had another 3 to go. Every day was different, chemo was a rollercoaster of emotions, a chemocoaster if you like. Some days were okay, some were like I wasn't even ill and just in the hospital for no reason, and the bad days, well they were hard. No, the bad days sucked.

Tuesday 16th May 2006 I was allowed home for a few hours in the afternoon, which I really enjoyed. When you are in hospital there is a limit to how much fun you can have. Then again, I wasn't there to have fun, I was there to get better. I was only at home for three hours, but it was worth

it. I treasured that time spent at home; I missed my own bed so much. Most importantly I missed my Mum's cooking. Even though on certain days it was painfully hard to eat with the mouth ulcers, I enjoyed it, even if it was just one or two bites from the meal.
Remember when I spoke about hair loss earlier on, and how that is what made me cry when being diagnosed? Well, that was something else...losing my thick, long hair.

Cancer.

Losing your hair. Losing my hair? Cancer?

Hair loss? I was going to lose my hair? I was going to go bald? No, this isn't right...are you sure you haven't messed up the results?

No?

CHAPTER 3

HAIR LOSS

Howard, you know – the guy from the Halifax advert.

Scarily enough I let my sister Vicky, BFATT and Sandee cut my hair. I had very long dark brown/black hair, which I loved and was proud of. They cut it to shoulder length after I was advised to cut it by a nurse who suggested it might be less of a shock when it started to fall out. My hair started to fall out around the 23rd of May 2006 which was a lot sooner than I thought it would be. I wasn't sure what to expect from any of this, so each day brought something new, whether it was good or bad. I hated that when I ran my fingers through my hair, clumps of it would be left in the palm of my hand. It was upsetting; I just wanted it to fall out completely, straight away, or not at all. It was so surreal when it started to fall out like that, I was too scared to wash it or get it wet when I was in the shower. I would have completely freaked out if it came out in one go, it was horrible. It was a shock losing my hair, I would wake up every morning and look at my pillow, collect all the hair from it and just sit and stare at it in my hand. I'm glad that's over but I'll never forget what that felt like. No one can even prepare you for it, even after you've been told it's a side effect of chemotherapy. I wasn't prepared. I didn't like this. It felt like I was losing my identity, losing a part of me, and I was afraid. Really afraid. Each day I felt like I was losing more and more of me, but my hair? Why?

Friday 26th May 2006 One of the nurses had mentioned that shaving all my hair off might be even less traumatic. Making it easier to take in, and there would be less hair to fall out. My cousin said he would do it for me, he had to sterilize all the components. I had no immune system; therefore, I was prone to get an infection. There was a lot of pressure on him. He did a great job and made me look cool. Or as BFATT said - "You look like Howard, you know. The guy from the Halifax advert".

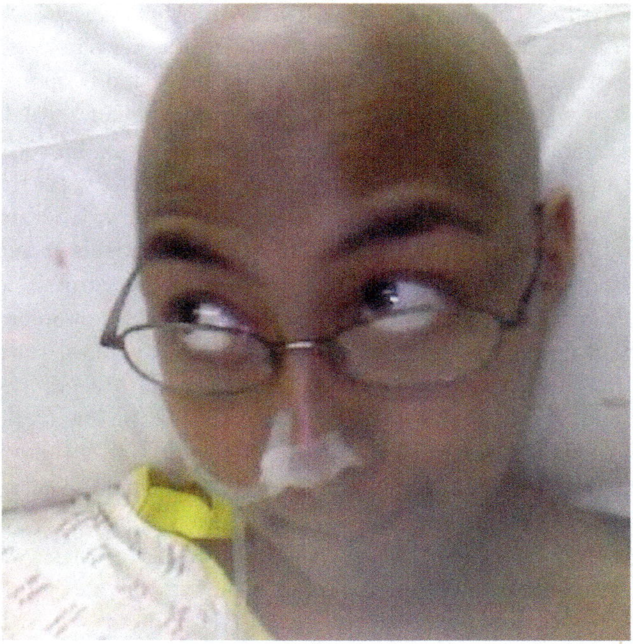

After he said that there was a slight pause. Which must've felt like hours to everyone in the room, they were seeing how I would react. I laughed, I laughed so much. We all had a chuckle out of it, and to be fair...he wasn't far off. What I soon discovered was not only was I okay with my bald head, but where the heck had those eyebrows been hiding?! I lost every single hair on my body, all but the brows. I think they look much more apparent here as they are the only parts of my head that had hair, either way it makes me chuckle now to look at that photo. So much brow, people pay for those bad boys! As well as losing the hair on my head, losing my eyelashes caused so many problems. They are there as a barrier, for protection; without them it is a struggle to open your eyes. I remember the heart-breaking morning when I couldn't open my eyes this one time, and I was so scared, I screamed. I screamed for help. My Mum calmed me down and said a nurse was on her way, they needed to wash my eyes as there was gunk over them, yes gunk. Appreciate your eyelashes guys because that feeling of waking up and not being able to open your eyes in what felt like forever was awful. Due to having no eyelashes the nurses had to clean my eyes each morning, just so they didn't become infected; also, so I could open my eyes and see. I spent a few mornings having to wait for them to clean my eyes so I could open them, it always felt like forever and each time I woke up like that I felt the same fear. My eyelashes grew back eventually, but they were finer hairs than they were before. I considered making new lashes out of my brows instead. I'm not too sure when that photo was taken, but I'm guessing between my first and second chemo as the mouth ulcers meant I was unable to eat properly, so I needed to have a feeding tube put in place; eurgh.

I didn't mind the shaved head once it was done, mainly because I discovered that it suited me. Or I was able to accept that this was how I had to be; this was me for now. Not forever, and that was okay. Whilst I talk about hair loss not lasting forever, let me share some old photos with you guys!

Here I am in 2006 with a bike seat cover on my face...because why not!? I love this photo because it is the last time, I recall ever being able to do a thumbs up with both hands. I'll not get to that part of my journey for a while as it's part of the stroke story, but it will make sense soon enough.

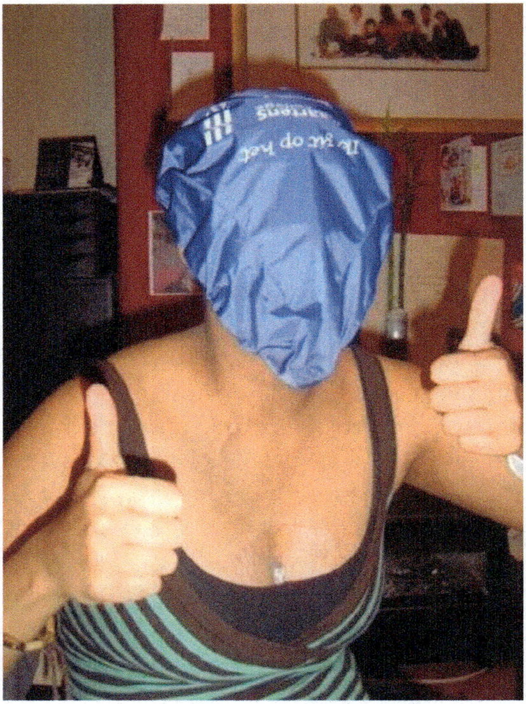

Also, that thing on my chest is the Groshong line that I spoke about earlier on. I loved that thing! I needed to be careful and make sure I didn't get it wet, as it could have caused an infection if not kept clean and well looked after.

Next up is me back in 2008, I was trying to remember how long it took to grow back, and here it is! At this stage of my hair growing back I was excited because it was growing back but I was also aware that I looked different, and people would judge me because of my short hair. Yes, I am eating a bowl of raw stuffing.

This was probably my favourite stage of my hair growing back because this is when I started to feel more like me again.

Before this stage though, we had the "Screech" stage (rest in peace)

Yup...so not only did I look like Howard when I was bald, I went on to look like Screech from Saved by the Bell. Yes, that is a Backstreet Boys CD and I still love them…and no I don't know why I am holding a rubber duck. I also loved the Screech reference.

HAIRRRR GLORIOUS HAIRRRRRR. Yup I love my hair.

The photo below was taken in August 2019, it's probably a bit longer now, but I think you've seen enough photos of my face for now.

I am super protective of my hair, so if you are a hairdresser and I ever come to you, I will perhaps come across as an awkward customer as my hair means a lot to me. You never fully appreciate things in your life until they are gone, and I appreciate the hell out of my hair. Especially as one of my biggest fears was to think it would never grow back. I usually only get it cut twice a year...and that is because I don't really like people near it. My hair, back off.

Back to hair loss, and the absolute CRAP feeling around it. There was a small part inside of me that felt empty, I used to wear a hat to and from hospital just so I could hide from the world, and the way people used to stare at me. The NHS arranged for me to meet someone who specialised in wigs for people who had lost their hair through chemotherapy. She handed me a booklet; I was with Sandee at the time so we both had a look through. I picked one that was pretty much the same as mine used to be before it was all cut away, perhaps a little lighter though. I picked one with a fringe as if my eyebrows were to fall out at least they would be covered (Haha didn't have to worry about the brows at all did I guys!?) The wig took about 5 days to come. I only wore it once. I remember wearing it to an appointment one day, just a routine check-up in between chemo courses. I took the wig off when I was sitting on a chair, it was so itchy, and I was aware I was wearing a wig; I was scared when people looked at me in case that they could tell it wasn't real. I took it off, and this lady looked at me in such a crazy way. Now looking back, how crazy might it be that maybe she thought it was my hair and not a wig, then staring in disbelief that I'd removed it. To that lady in the waiting room – I'm sorry if I gave you an evil glare, but my head was hot, and I feared you looking at me in the fragile state that I was in. That same day, there was a little boy who said to his Mum ever so softly, but loud enough that I could make it out "Mummy, that girl has taken her hair off". That women told her son something that made me smile "I don't think she's feeling very well, I wish I could take mine off". Haha, to think she wished that. Who knows, maybe even hers was a wig and she didn't want to scare her son. Well, I scared him for her. Me and my lil' egg head. I wore hats to and from the hospital, when I was home, I didn't wear anything unless my head was cold. I didn't feel myself when my hair was gone, everything just seemed cruel, and I didn't know if I was getting better or worse. Believe me when I say people stare, it could be a harmless glance, but

anytime a stranger looked at me, I felt this sympathetic sorrow and I hated that look. Screw you. Look at someone else. If you are going through this you might not even care, these days I care very little of what others think about me, unless its people close to me.
18-year-old, bald Howard-looking Leena, cared. I cared an awful lot, not only did I have an illness that, at the start wasn't visible unless you knew, but I also now cannot hide from you, the world, that yes - I'm ill.

Yes.

I am a cancer patient.

CHAPTER 4

THROWING UP

This part of the book is about the second stage of chemotherapy treatment in particular, the infections that I was run down with due to no immune system to protect me against infections and an insight into how hard it really was for me. Anything in *italics* throughout this book are my thoughts or have been taken from a diary that I wrote whilst having treatment in 2006.

Sunday 28th May 2006: in hospital with my first infection

Currently on a drip for platelets as my platelet count is low, my temperature has settled down to 36°C. BFATT stayed with me last night, think he's staying tonight too. I want a Gregg's Chicken Bake so badly and a Domino's, chicken wings from Domino's, heavenly.

As always food was on my mind...junk food. I had completely lost my appetite at this point, but a girl can dream. Did I mention I like food?
After each course of chemo, I was allowed to go home until I was due the next batch of chemo. I needed to check my temperature several times throughout the day whilst I was at home. The reason I needed to monitor my temperature was

due to possible infection. If my temperature was too high (over 39°C) I would have needed to go back into hospital straight away so that they could give me antibiotics. It could be as simple as a common cold, for example if someone had a cold and had been near me, I would pretty much have caught it in a matter of seconds and my body had no way of protecting me from the bacteria.
Having an infection delayed the next course of chemo, which meant I had to be in hospital a bit longer until I finished the course of antibiotics.
If anyone wanting to visit me had a cold, or any symptoms such as a sniffly nose, they needed to stay the hell away. I tell you now, if you are going through chemo and you are given a set of rules and guidelines, FOLLOW THEM. Follow every single little detail because it will make things a little bit easier. This is going to be quite a journey for you, you will have good days and bad days however, my bad days outweighed the good.

Some of my rules were as follows:

NO TAKEAWAYS

YOU WHAT?! This was due to preparation and not knowing who had handled the food, the risk of passing on bacteria was too high. No KFC for me.

NO UNWRAPPED SWEETS

WHAT! Yup, no Pic 'n mix for Leena. This was again due to bacteria and germs, and not knowing who had been handling them. Too risky!

NO NUTS, CHOCOLATE WITH NUTS, POPCORN, FRESH MAYO, CHEESE SUCH AS MOZZARELLA, BRIE, FETA, NO CAKES

WITH CREAM, ICE CREAM FROM ICE CREAM VANS, PATE, PRAWNS, SHELLFISH, SMOKED SALMON, SALAD, SKINS ON JACKET POTATOES, ICE FROM ICE MAKING MACHINES, HERBAL TEA...

I can't really remember each reason as to why I wasn't allowed these, but the main things were anything unwrapped or non-pasteurised. I was allowed crisps. So, thank you for allowing me that, Mr. Chemo. Not being able to eat so many things and to be given a list of things I had to avoid was initially quite overwhelming, but I lost my appetite as time went on and some days, I was even too exhausted from the treatment to even be able to chew.

Saturday 3rd June 2006:

So yesterday I had a really bad day, I didn't feel right just before we went to the hospital. I had to go into hospital for the routine check-up in between treatments. They take my blood, take my temperature and that lil obs machine was wheeled over to me. From the blood tests they can see if I need a blood transfusion, platelets, or if I have caught any kind of infection. If my temperature was above 39°C I would have to stay in hospital once a bed became available. My temperature being higher than this would have meant that I had an infection, due to no white cells and no immune system whatsoever.

As I was leaving the hospital, I threw up everywhere...oops, just got home and I've just generally felt down all day.

I vividly remember being mid-text to Sandee whilst throwing up...multi-tasking at its finest. I was feeling bad the whole day, up until and after my check-up. The side effects are horrible and can happen anytime or any day, whether it be 4am or whether it be right in the middle of the ward just as you are leaving to go home.

I remember this day SO WELL. Mum was laughing at me afterwards for texting whilst throwing up. My Dad took my phone off me so I could compose my vomiting self. There was A LOT of it. I remember thinking *'oh no, I'm going to be sick, I think it's going to travel far'*. All the nurses and cleaners cleaned up after me, I asked my Mum if I could help them as it was my sick and I was embarrassed. One nurse called JP politely reminded me that I am the patient, and they are there to look after me. I threw up a lot during my treatment, and it never got easier, I never got used to it. It sucked. It made me feel weak, it made strangers look at me with their concerning eyes, it made me feel helpless.

<u>Monday 12th June, second stage of chemo:</u>

I was put on an open ward with two other patients during my 2nd stage of chemo. I didn't like it one bit, I enjoy being in a place I can call my own. When I had a side room, in a way it was my own and I had my privacy. By the second day of treatment, I had my own room again, it brought back memories of my 1st stage of treatment as it was the same room - Ward 62, Room 4, Level G.

During my treatment the world cup was on, I pretty much watched every match. I've never really been a fan of football, but I had to make sure I watched every single match, I'm pretty sure the whole ward watched it. I can remember hearing the men from the ward next-door shouting and sighing when the ball went in the goal, or near it. It was pretty good to watch, and it took my mind off everything. It was like nothing was wrong, until all the machines started beeping bringing you back to the harsh reality. Although after a bit of time looking at the machine in more depth, I did find a button that muted that annoying beeping sound, so as soon as I knew a nurse had heard it, I whacked that button in a hurry.

My Dad has always enjoyed watching football. BFATT and my Dad would often watch the matches together. My Dad and BFATT are Arsenal supporters and that's why I've fallen to follow them as a team. Now I may not know everything or anything there is to know about football, but what I do know is that I love to watch it. I LOVE IT. It pulled me through one of the hardest times of my life and so it will forever put a smile on my face, even when yes, my team lose. It is sort of a family tradition now, me, my Mum and Dad all sit around the TV to watch it. Yes, I'm an Arsenal fan, no you can't change my mind. Yes, we can watch football together, and yes you can make fun of me because my friends Stu and Luke most certainly do, I hear you guys.

The four stages of chemo were different doses and went over a certain number of days. The first treatment was 10 days long, the last two were 5 days. I can't remember exactly how long the second treatment was, but I think it was roughly around 7 days. The chemo was such a high dose for the second course that they needed to be a few hours apart. So, if one dose was delayed it would mean that a nurse would have to come and change it over in the middle of the night, which was the case on most of my treatments. I can still hear that annoying beeping noise from the drip stand, when you hear that at 3am, which was usually around the time I had fallen asleep...it was enough to make anyone go insane. It's even worse when you are on the open ward as the other patients' machines are going off too. It was like beep after beep after frickin' beep.

The first treatment went by quickly considering it was the longest of the four stages. The 2nd stage dragged on a bit, but luckily, I had everyone around me, and a TV!

With everyone that I had around me, it made things so much easier. I had someone with me every moment of everyday. Everyone was really supportive, and they still are. I don't think they realise how much they helped me get through cancer, I can't imagine how hard it must have been visiting someone close to you, especially in the state that I was in. Lying there completely drained of life in a hospital bed with needles in my arm, machines beeping, my hair falling out, tablets in a pot in front of me and a chart to measure my intake and outtake, gross.

I will admit that at times I did get annoyed with people always being there, I couldn't help it, my emotions were all over the place. I was annoyed at myself for even feeling this way but there was a lot going on and the time I spent in hospital made me live through every single emotion, the good, the bad and the ugly. Without my friends and family, I would never have got through this time of my life. Thank you for putting up with me and for understanding how I was feeling, or for trying to. There were moments where I didn't even have time to realise how ill I was, and times I'd lie awake at stupid o' clock listening to the beeping noise of the machine or hearing the nurses rushing about their station. The moments where I was alone, even for a split second is what made me realise where I was. I was an 18-year-old, lying in a hospital bed, with several IV drips surrounding my bed and pumping chemo into my body because I was a cancer patient. I had cancer. It has become so much easier as time has gone on to talk about it, and to look back at what I have overcome. I hope you are reading this knowing that you can get through this, you can get through anything just have hope. Use the support of those around you, let them help you through If you are unable to get yourself through this time, you do not have to fight alone. If you need help, ask for help. If you need a hug, have a hug! If you need to cry, cry. Believe me, I cry a lot. They could be happy tears, they could be sad tears, they could be tears for no reason, or they could be tears because I've just watched The Lion King. Since suffering from the stroke, I cry a lot, my emotions are hard to control, and crying is something I wish I could control but I am alive and if it is something I must live with, I'll make it my own.

Most importantly when you can, smile. I feel that I am a much stronger person today, it has made me respect and appreciate life so much more. I'm closer to my friends and family that were around me then and are still around me now.

CHAPTER 5

DOCTOR ROGER EVELY

They say patients need rest but it is almost impossible to get. You want rest, but by the time you get to sleep you are woken by nurses having to take your blood or by a cleaner mopping the floor. Being in hospital is the most exhausting time, not only does cancer drain everything out of you, but it is a mission to get more than 4 hours of sleep overnight.

Well, that was my case anyway.

On the 13th of June 2006 I was seen by Dr Evely, he was very pleased with my progress and talked me through what would happen after my 3rd chemo. I would have to have a bone marrow harvest where they would collect my stem cells and freeze them in case I needed them in the future.

I had an infection after every stage of chemo, which they said was to be expected but the infection after the 4th stage of chemo led onto something I'll never forget.

A few weeks after my 2nd chemo I had a bone marrow test whilst I was awake. Now I understand why I was sedated the first few times; it was the worst feeling ever. OUCH.
Try to imagine a needle going into your back, into your hip

bone...it has to go in so deep that it sucks a sample of the bone through a syringe. However, they need to collect more than just one, they take several samples. You can't actually hear it out loud, however it's such a bizarre sensation that you can hear it within your body. People that have had this done before will be able to relate, it isn't nice. I never really got used to them and I screamed and cried during them, especially when they had to be redone so often. My body was so sore from the previous tests, but I knew it had to be done and knew they would be over soon. I had to have the bone marrow biopsies every three months at this point, I always pictured a pneumatic drill going into my back. Horrid, I know but it's exactly how it felt to me. For those of you that don't know bone marrow tests are done so they can see whether there are cancer cells in the bone marrow. They take samples and look at them in a lab under their microscopes.
Now I don't want to scare you if this is something that you perhaps might have to have yourself if you are reading this, this is just how it was for me. My pain threshold was apparently pretty good; however, I think they told me this before I screamed. I won't make it up and say it was a breeze because it was very uncomfortable, however, once you have had one you know what to expect and can prepare yourself for the next one. You'll probably have one and be like *'what the hell was that Leena girl crying about, this is nothing'* and I hope that you have that experience…however, if it is a similar sensation to what I went through, I feel your pain; I really do, but you've got this!

Monday 31st July 2006 3:10pm

This is when my 3rd stage of chemo began. The drug that would be working alongside the chemo was a strange orange/red colour, which was well weird as whenever I went to the toilet my urine was bright orange, yuck. The treatment lasted five days, and as always it was the longest 5 days ever.

5th August 2006 1:40pm

I had a heart ultrasound scan. They applied a gel around the area of my heart, it was freezing! It was really weird seeing my heart on a screen to the left of me and hearing it was quite different, I don't know what I expected it to sound like but I was quite amazed by the sound as it was almost like footsteps along a dark and echoed corridor.

By 'heart ultrasound scan', the medical term for this is an 'Echocardiogram.'

This chapter is titled after a man who is an absolute legend - Doctor Roger Evely, aka Dr Evely. Not only was this man the guy that had to deliver the bad news to me, my family, and my friends on the 8th of May 2006, but he was the most amazing consultant and an absolute hero, I was incredibly lucky to have him as my doctor. He will probably never see this book; I hope he does because he saved my life. Him and his team, every single nurse, every single doctor, even the kitchen staff, in fact every single person that stepped foot to work within the walls of the Oncology in Bristol during May 2006 – 2011, thank you. From the absolute bottom of my heart, thank you. You made my journey so much easier, the care you gave me was simply beautiful. Thank you for making the worst time of my life all that much better. Thank you for letting me have my family stay over, for relaxing the visiting hours so that I never had to be alone, and for putting up with me having so many visitors each day. Dr Ray, you also need recognition - for being the only doctor to do my Bone Marrow tests with me having the least amount of pain possible, even if it was 99% painful, it was better than 100% pain.

Dr Evely. Thank you for saving my life.

CHAPTER 6

FROSTIES

<u>Wednesday 30th August 2006 7:17am</u>

The 3rd stage of chemo wasn't too bad apart from having a belly ache for two days.

The kitchen staff ask you what you would like for breakfast and it's on your side table by about 7:30am. Hospital food is really not the best, so when my immune system was getting stronger, I got my Mum to bring me some homemade food, yum.

EVERY morning since I was in Ward 62 for treatment, I had Kellogs Frosties. The odd day when there was a fry up available on the menu I jumped at that chance, but it was mainly Frosties. Whenever I had really bad mouth ulcers it was unbelievably painful to chew or swallow anything, so I had to have soggy Frosties.

I'm glad to say I am now sick of the sight of them and haven't eaten them since. I had them EVERY single morning for roughly 5 months and that's a whole lotta' Frostie.

I've been in hospital with a really horrid infection, the worst yet. It has been horrible; I didn't eat for two weeks, so the nurses have had to put a tube down my nose to feed me, which goes straight into my stomach. I'm now eating and I'm able to walk to the toilet on my own. I go home in the afternoons now and have dinner at home which is A LOT nicer than hospital food.

That feeding tube was so gross; I couldn't eat as I had so many ulcers and blisters in my mouth which were due to the infection and my weakened immune system. The side effects hit me this time around, I couldn't even stand the sight of food without feeling sick. Even drinking water through a straw proved difficult. Luckily the feeding tube was taken out as over the next two weeks I started to get my appetite back. I remember not being able to walk as the chemo had drained everything out of me, so I had my family or BFATT there to help me walk to the toilet, also helping me on and off it. I had to sit down to brush my teeth as I couldn't stand up very long, and there were times where my Mum even had to brush them for me. I can't read my writing in the diary I kept but what I can make out seems like they may have not needed to give me the 4th and final treatment, they weren't sure whether it would be necessary in case it made me more ill. However, due to an infection I came down with they had to carry on the treatment.

Thursday 5th October 2006

So, I've been at home pretty much a month now, I went into hospital Sunday night (01/10/06) they were supposed to be doing a Bone Marrow Harvest to collect my stem cells on the Monday, but it had to be cancelled as there were too many emergencies on the ward. So now it has been rescheduled for 08/10/06, I'll be staying that night and having the Bone Marrow Harvest the following morning. Depending on how I feel after the bone marrow test, they will start my last lot of treatment. Like my 3rd treatment this dose of chemo will last for 5 days.

Looking back over my diary and reminiscing I would like to

say that going through this was an absolute nightmare, the worst nightmare. Even after all this time I can tell you that it gives you a completely different outlook on life. I've become a lot closer to my friends, family and it brought me and BFATT closer together. The friends I had then, are still my close friends today. Despite them being at college back then or working or simply having their own lives to live – they always made time to see me. If they were unable to see me for a few days, they would always send me a text or ask my family how I was doing. All my friends, my family, BFATT, people at college that I hardly knew all made an effort to check in on me, so I thank you. Check in on one another, care for each other always.

When something so big and something that has such a massive impact on not only myself but those closest to me, it naturally brings you closer. It also makes you realise the people that matter, and I was lucky because it appeared, I mattered to a lot of people. It made me appreciate my parents a lot more, of course I still throw a tantrum like a 16-year-old at times, but that's just me...we all have our moments. I love their company; I would be so lost without them. They were there for me every single day and they mean the world to me. I've not forgotten you siblings! Angel, Vicky & Ricki thank you for being you and for also getting me through the crap times. You guys are the best siblings anyone could ever ask for and I'm very grateful that I get to be your little sister.

One of the main things that I felt going through treatment was that I wanted to feel normal, and to be treated like nothing was wrong, even though I was in a bad way. Having so many people around me it helped push what I was going through to the back of my mind, and I felt pretty 'normal' despite being very ill. Everyone around me helped me remain positive throughout my journey and keeping positive is what gets me through each day. Not every day is a good day, we are all human and sometimes you just need a bit of time out, but I am happy to be alive and I owe that to all of you. So, if you are reading this and things are too much with whatever it is you are going through, speak to someone about it. You are allowed to feel more than one emotion during this treatment, or just in general. If like me, at times you may feel empty, you are allowed to feel empty. I felt empty for a long time, but I had friends and family to pick me back up when I needed it. The key is to know that what you feel will pass, but I can't promise you won't feel like that again. What I can, and I CAN absolutely reassure you is that one day will be the greatest day, and that day will be when you feel 'you' again. I can't tell you how long it will take to get that feeling back and if you are lucky, you may actually not lose that feeling throughout your treatment, but hold on, keep fighting and smile.

Throw up, smile again, cry and smile after. If you are feeling empty, surround yourself with those who can make you smile.

CHAPTER 7

DEAL OR NO DEAL?

Tuesday 10th October

I had my bone marrow test yesterday morning and I'm in a bit of pain, it makes moving from place to place pretty difficult. They are starting my last course of treatment tomorrow; it will be for five days. I'm already missing food from home and home in general. Hopefully if things go to plan, I'll be home by Monday or Tuesday. I hope this pain goes away too.

Thinking back to this day, I don't think I quite realised how close to the end of treatment I was and what an amazing time this should have been. I do remember thinking *is it the end?* If so, maybe I have to feel really bad before I feel better again? Some part of me had a bad feeling, just because of how bad the most recent infection was. I really am unsure how to explain how bad and run down I felt, so to put it bluntly it felt like I was dying.

12:48pm Wednesday 11th October. Day 1, room 6

My chemo starts around 6pm. There will be two lots of chemo in the morning and one at night, I think. It may be the other way around. The bone marrow site is still painful but isn't as sore. Me and Mum are just watching some lame game show on TV. These days will hopefully go by faster than I expect, I just can't stand the food and the long space of time between each treatment.

The TV show me and Mum were watching was called 'Deal or No Deal'. Getting money just for picking a box, what!?

All the hospital staff were amazing as always during this time. When I lost my appetite, they always tried to find something that I might be able to eat, but my mouth was so full of ulcers that I couldn't eat anything, even if I wanted to. I got to the point that I couldn't eat at all and so they had to put the feeding tube back in for a few months. I missed being able to eat real food and feeling that tube going into my nose was disgusting and surreal. This was the second time that I had the tube put in, and it's not a pleasant memory remembering what it was like when they had to take the last one out. I had to take a deep breath in, whilst the nurse pulled it out, gag. I remember one of the nurses Sheryll.
Now, lovely readers let me tell you about Sheryll. She was absolutely devoted to her duties as a nurse. She treated everyone, every single person with the most care you could possibly want as a patient, and I adored her. She is Filipino, and with my Mum being Filipino it meant that they would have chit chats in Tagalog whilst they were changing my bed or whilst Sheryll was getting my medication ready. Sheryll could tell how much I really wanted to eat during one of many days that I had blisters in my mouth but was unable to, she suggested satsumas and ice lollies once and said it may not be so painful eating those. I tried it and I became obsessed with eating satsumas, clementines & oranges...until these also became too painful to eat. Next up...ice lollies!!

Twisters and Calippos. Hell yes. Firstly, these are both so small now?! Back then I'd eat a whole pack in a few days, now I'd need ten packs. Secondly, I praise you Sheryll for this suggestion because Calippos were the greatest idea for my blister ridden mouth.

My parents bumped into Sheryll in a supermarket not long ago, sometime in December I believe, and I hope I get that chance because we are going to go and eat some ice lollies. Ten packs of them.

I remember my nephew Luke visiting me in hospital, he would have been 7 years old at the time. He looked so scared as I didn't have any hair and would have looked so much different to the last time that he saw me. He said hello to me from the corridor as I was too ill to have anyone in my room, I also remember him waving and saying, "Hi Leena." I always thought it was so brave of him to do that if you're reading this dude – thanks for coming to see me!

He never calls me Aunty, because well that makes me feel weird and old, I'm too cool for that...He's now 24! Me and Luke spoke about him visiting me when I was ill a few months ago and he said he remembered the day clearly. He said he wasn't sure what to expect but he wanted to see me. So, thanks mate, hope I didn't freak you out too much with my bald head.

I really loved writing in my diary and using that as a place to escape. Often now I still write things down or keep a journal, even if it's a quick note on my phone. There is just something about doing this that helps me keep at ease or helps with any anxiety I have at the time. It's really interesting to think about how we each deal with things. Some of us often think by ignoring our emotions and feelings that we are dealing with it, but trust me when I say keeping so much bottled up for longs periods of time is so unhealthy, if you can just write down how you feel or just speak and open up that little bit to someone it will make you feel a little bit better, you might not think it at the time, but it really helps.

Plus, I do like to talk a lot which is very useful to fill a book it turns out…

The last thing I wrote in my diary back in 2006 was the below.

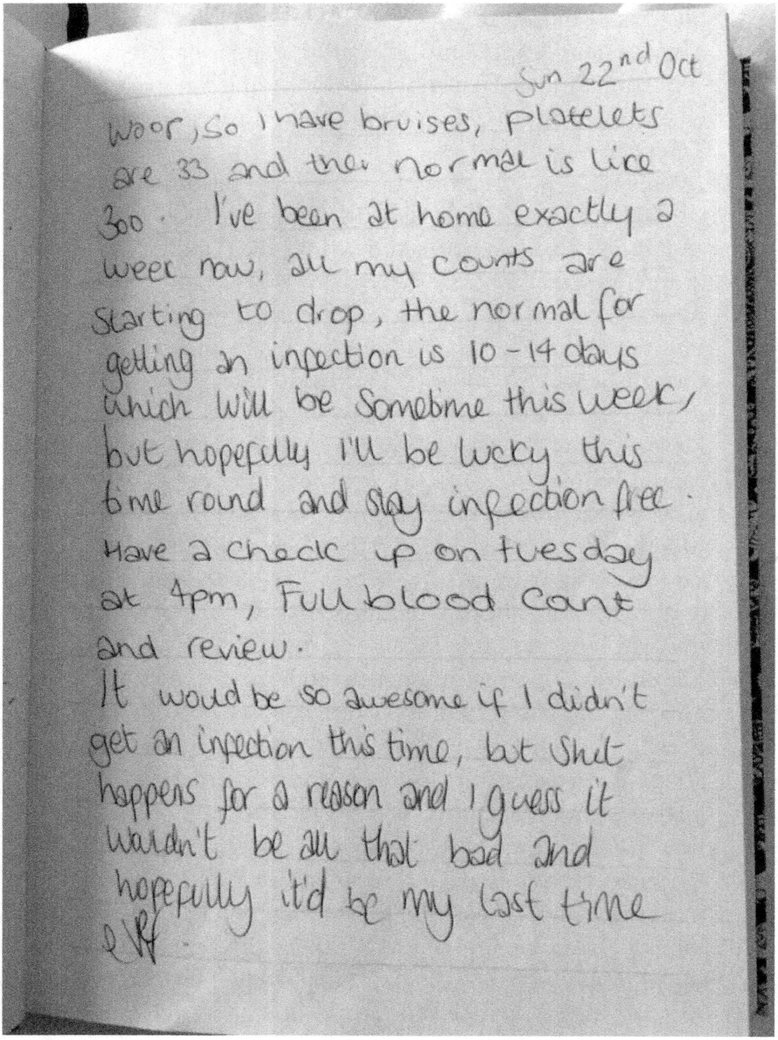

Sun 22nd Oct

Woor, So I have bruises, platelets are 33 and the normal is like 300. I've been at home exactly a week now, all my counts are starting to drop, the normal for getting an infection is 10-14 days which will be sometime this week, but hopefully I'll be lucky this time round and stay infection free. Have a check up on tuesday at 4pm, Full blood count and review.

It would be so awesome if I didn't get an infection this time, but shit happens for a reason and I guess it wouldn't be all that bad and hopefully it'd be my last time eVa.

I know my writing isn't the greatest, it's worse now...but within good reason which I'll explain eventually.

So, if it's unclear, please read this bit instead:

"Woop, so I have bruises, platelets are 33 and the normal is like 300. I've been at home exactly a week now, all my counts are starting to drop, the normal for getting an infection is 10-14 days which will be sometime this week, but hopefully I'll be lucky this time round and stay infection free. I have a check up on Tuesday at 4pm, full blood count and review. It would be awesome if I didn't get an infection this time, but shit happens for a reason, and I guess it wouldn't be all that bad and hopefully it'd be my last time ever."

Firstly, sorry for swearing Mum and Dad.

Secondly, this is the last blood test that I remember having, I love how I started this diary entry with a "woop", ever so positive even whilst having crap results. My blood counts were monitored frequently, a normal platelet count is 150-450. When I was first diagnosed, I believe my platelet count was basically non-existent, so 33 wasn't the worst it had ever been...but it obviously wasn't ideal and meant that I was still ill and on the mend.
Just to give a bit of clarity and understanding to this diary note, chemotherapy kills everything.
By this I mean it basically kills your good cells and your bad cells (the cancerous ones). After each course of chemo your immune system is at zero, it is completely shut down. Therefore, after each chemotherapy course it meant that I was prone to catch an infection. After each of my 4 chemo treatments I got ill. By this I mean I caught an infection which needed treatment in the form of antibiotics in hospital through a drip. There was a lot of going back and forth to the Oncology. I spent more time there than I did at home,

but that was the place I needed to get better. Even knowing it was where I needed to be didn't mean I didn't miss home; I missed a lot of things. The infection after my fourth and final chemo was the worst. The absolute worst. Looking over that last line "It would be awesome if I didn't get an infection this time" and "it wouldn't be all that bad" it couldn't have been so far from the truth.

Not only was it the worst, but it also completely broke me.

CHAPTER 8

PNEUMONIA

I went back to the Oncology ward after my last course of chemo, as I usually would after each course. I sat next to a lady who had pneumonia, now I didn't know this at the time; I just saw an empty chair and went to sit in it. I overheard the doctor telling her what was wrong and what they think she may have. My Dad was sitting on the opposite side of the room and told me to sit by him as there were no other patients sitting over that side of the room. He wanted me to move because he could see how unwell the lady was and didn't want me at risk of getting more ill with my low immune system. The only reason I didn't move was because I felt it would have been a bit rude had I moved away from her, I wish I had listened to my Dad and moved because I caught pneumonia off the lady. Not only that but it was completely downhill from this moment, all for sitting innocently in a waiting room after all my chemo was **finally** complete. Little did I know that my battle was about to begin all over again, this time it was a fight for my **life**.
After the nurses took my blood, a few moments later I remember suddenly feeling very unwell, but these were new symptoms. They were different to how I usually felt in between treatments. This was the check up after my last

chemo, I guess I was hoping I'd get lucky this time round and feel okay.

Unfortunately, I was wrong.

I remember lying in a bed on the outpatient ward with a drip and three blankets over me...I was freezing. I was shaking and struggling to breathe. I spent a bit of time in the day area until they got a bed ready for me. I was moved to a side room, and I was given an oxygen mask. I just remember crawling into the blankets, I must have had about five blankets by this point. I curled up into a ball hoping this feeling would pass, it didn't. I don't think I knew what was going on at this point, I just knew THIS was the worst infection and I hoped it would go away. I was just so cold and uncomfortable. After being on Ward 62 for a while, I wasn't getting any better. A doctor spoke to me about moving to the BRI, HDU (High Dependency Unit). I said no as I didn't want to move; I had been on that ward for 6 months and I wasn't prepared for change, I didn't like the thought of new faces at all. All the doctors and nurses knew me on Ward 62, it was a safe place to be. The doctor assured me it would be the best thing to do as they didn't have the equipment needed to make me better, and so I had no choice but to move. I hoped the HDU would make me feel better soon, *I just can't breathe.*

The BRI (Bristol Royal Infirmary) is situated back-to-back with the Oncology Centre, it just meant me having to be pushed on my bed through endless corridors with those horrible ceiling lights.

Before the move I had a different oxygen mask put on, it scared the hell out of me. It was fastened onto my face, and it was so tight. I felt like Hannibal Lecter. The mask was tightened at the back of my head and pulled very, very tightly. It made my mouth dry, I felt like crying over and over again. I didn't want this on my face; however, I needed it as I wasn't able to breathe without it.

I was taken by the porter to the BRI with my Mum and Dad. I also think BFATT, my sisters and brother came up shortly after as well. When we arrived at HDU I saw a bed inside a room with LOADS of machines, there were louder beeps than Ward 62, oxygen masks were draping over the back of the bed, it was dark and scary. I wasn't looking forward to spending any time there. I don't want to be in there, it felt like the walls were closing in on me and I was scared.

Please can I go home?

From the moment of seeing the room right up until I was affected by a stroke, I can only vaguely remember what happened, please excuse anything that may seem disjointed and out of place in this chapter. I will do my best to piece it together in the best way that I can, so thank you for reading and staying with me on this one, it will be the hardest chapter to write.

I will always remember my Mum and Dad asking the nurses if it would be possible for my Mum to stay with me throughout the day and night, but there wasn't any space in the room; there was only just enough space for people to be stood in there, or for the nurses to come in and check on me. The room was very compact, full of machines, full of loads of medical equipment, full of emptiness and loneliness. *Please can I go home?*

The nurses said that unfortunately no one would be able to stay in the room with me overnight. This really upset me as I was so used to having someone with me during the entire duration of my chemotherapy, to hear them say no was a shock. I didn't want to be alone. I was scared.

This is where things get a little hazy. I think my parents were advised to go home and get some rest as it had been a very full-on day, and no one had slept or eaten. I was in the right place to get better, and I suppose there wasn't anything they could do. Even though the nurses had said they couldn't stay in my room, they did let them know that they were welcome anytime to stay in the family room, which was nearby, just so that they could take it in turns to come and see me. I'm not sure if everyone went home, or if anyone had stayed behind before this next part, which will always be one of my worst memories. However, I am alive and well, and memories are what shape us, and I am lucky to still have my memory so I will be forever grateful.

I remember a nurse asking if I would like a drink, he was very kind and he could tell that I was scared. I don't believe I spoke, but I politely nodded. I didn't talk at all when I was in the HDU, mainly because the oxygen mask dried my throat out when I tried, but also because I was completely scared. There was so much going on and I was overwhelmed. I didn't recognise any of the staff and I was simply just scared and lost.

I hadn't been alone since being diagnosed with Leukaemia and I didn't like the thought of my Mum not being able to stay with me. The nurse came in with some blackcurrant squash in a plastic cup, I was so thirsty. I remember that I wasn't allowed to take the mask off, and it usually took 1 or 2 nurses to remove it for me, so I had to drink it through a straw that I was able to fit through a gap in the mask. Something strange happened when I went to pick up the cup. I had a few sips, but when I went to put it back on the table my hand just dropped it, I couldn't control what I was doing. I don't remember letting go, *what happened?*

I couldn't control my arm. These are the last few things that I can remember about that moment. I heard the machines beeping even louder and more erratic. I could hear the nurses shouting and then, I saw my right arm drooping beside me. Everything went dark. Everything was empty and I was alone, I was alone now more than ever. Then there were bright white lights and shadows over me, everything was blurry.

Where am I?

Then nothing.

Now I am awake.

I am in a different room.

Hello?

Where am I?

Hello?

What's happened?

Hello?

Why can't I talk?

Hello?

Whose arm is that?

Hello?

Whose legs are those?

Hello?

Why can't I move?

Hello?

Why can't you hear me?

Hello?

Hello?

Hello?

CHAPTER 9

I'VE HAD A STROKE?

The memories I have between the HDU (High Dependency Unit) and the ICU (Intensive Care Unit) are vivid at points but there are moments that I cannot recall at all or piece together. These moments were when I perhaps slipped away into what felt like how I imagine it would feel like to die. The moments after hearing all the beeping and after hearing several nurses and doctors amongst my hospital bed drifted away. These sounds drifted away so quickly that I remember feeling trapped somewhere, but I didn't know where I was or how to get out. I was unable to move forward or to step back into my body. It is as if I was out of my body, but I couldn't see anyone or hear anything anymore, I just felt like I didn't belong where I was, in this lonely place. I remember lying on the bed and being moved to the ICU, I don't quite remember how it all fits together and after all this time I am not sure I want to know.

This by far is the most upsetting part to write and to re-live. Writing about it is one thing but thinking about it is still hard. It always will be, it was tough. Tough isn't even the right word. There are no words to fully explain to you how hard this time of my life was and still is. To look at me you might think I have fully healed from the stroke, or you might not even know that it is something that I went through or still deal with day to day. Unless you know me, or unless you are reading this, I don't believe you would ever know. In fact, people that know me might not even be aware, because I don't like to make a big deal out of it. There are people worse off in the world than me, but that's not to say I didn't and don't have my own battles. I am lucky. I am lucky to be here. I will always be grateful that I made it out the other side, but it still is tough being a cancer survivor, it is even harder to be a stroke survivor.

When I say it's tough being a cancer survivor don't take that the wrong way, if you have survived cancer, it is so badass and I am proud of you and of myself, of course I am. There is something I often struggle with and that is 'Survivor's Guilt'. It is an incredible thing that I fought and won my battle, but unfortunately sometimes that isn't the case; even if you are the strongest in the fight, sometimes you lose.

Not being able to ask what has happened to you is crazy, I don't think I understood what had happened at the time or what was happening. I was told multiple times, on several occasions each day, but my mind was all over the place, and I was scared. I didn't know what time, day, or even what month it was and I'm sure at one point I was confused by the name 'Leena', my own name. Seeing several drips at the end of my bed, one or two bags of blood, the other platelets, needles in and out of my right arm. At this point I couldn't even feel the right side of my body, I was unaware that the arm drooping next to me was in fact **my** arm. My brain had switched off the fact that I had two arms. It was so surreal, I kept trying to move away from the arm, but it was mine and I couldn't move much anyway. I was just about able to move my head. From this point I was not left alone, my Mum, Dad and my family made sure of that. My parents stayed with me 24/7, if they had to leave the room it would've only been if one of my siblings or BFATT was present.

My hospital bed faced the window, I could see when it was

dark or light, but I still never knew what time of the day it was, what's worse is I was unable to ask and that frustrated me so much. I remember Angel & Vicky coming in with magazines, reading me all the latest gossip. I couldn't even smile at this point. Everything they read to me was going in one ear and out the other; I couldn't concentrate for more than a couple of seconds. I don't remember sleeping at all, not once. Apparently, I was asleep most of the time, but I don't remember it feeling like that. I felt like I had been awake nonstop for 3 months, or longer. It felt like a lifetime, and I was scared. I was lost.

I remember Mum and Dad doing their "shift" to stay by my bedside. They used to massage my feet and legs to help the circulation; I couldn't feel any of it. I couldn't feel my legs, I remember looking down thinking *whose legs are those? Why are someone else's legs in my bed?* It seems silly that I thought this at the time, like who else's legs could they have been? However, it truly was scary not to recognise your own body as being yours. It was the lowest I have ever felt in my life. I thought cancer was bad, this really and I mean really, sucked. The stroke happened in November 2006, once all my chemo treatment was over. There was a clot on the left side of my brain; the left side of your brain controls the right side of your body. I was unable to move my right arm; I was also paralysed from the waist down. I was only able to move my head, my left arm; and only able to move my upper body with help. I was unable to speak or do any facial expressions. I was unable to eat, unable to chew, swallow food and unable to drink. Due to not being able to eat or drink I had my best pal the feeding tube back in. As I was unable to move or get myself to a bathroom, I also had a catheter put in for all the wees. As for number 2s, well when you are unable to get someone's attention because you **CANNOT** speak, let's just say at 18 years of age pooing yourself is the lowest of lows. I was unable to get anyone's attention if I did need to go as I couldn't speak, also in the early days as I had no feeling down there, I didn't even know if I had gone. I couldn't press the buzzer as it was on the wrong side, which my family later mentioned to the staff who then moved it to the left side of my body (my "good" side). By the time I had managed to tell my brain to press that button it was always too late anyway, and that was it. I was simply telling my brain to press the button. My brain was having none of it.

In the early stages of the stroke, even my left arm struggled as it was my non-dominant hand and I was struggling to cope with everything going on, I just didn't understand. My brain wasn't letting me understand what was going on. My brain wasn't fully functioning, so it was all a bit traumatic. I remember thinking back to the chemo treatment and how much help I needed during that time. I remember feeling really embarrassed when I needed help washing and doing day to day tasks because I was just too weak to do these daily tasks by myself. Little did I know it would get a whole heap worse when I physically became unable to do anything and I mean anything. I needed to rely on others, I was useless. I was lost. I won't apologise to you reading this if it is too graphic because this is what happened, and it sucked. Big time.

I had a very bizarre obsession with ice, I used to get hot one minute and then seconds later freezing cold. Someone had thought of an idea to get a pad of paper and a pen so I could communicate that way. I went to write the word 'ice' once and I couldn't spell it. My brain was so confused, I was confused, I couldn't remember why I was even holding a pen. I wrote "ce" first, then I wrote "I" about 4 minutes later, it wasn't legible either.

After writing it, I got really upset as I didn't remember writing it, I didn't recognise my own writing and I had forgotten in a split second what I was trying to write or ask my family. I had to do all this with my left hand, which my brain had just about worked out was part of my body. My brain was still learning and re-wiring, so it was difficult to write and even more annoying to work out what I was going to write once my pen was on the paper. When my family and BFATT eventually worked out what it said I rubbed my fingertips together. It then became our own made-up sign language.

I don't think I have ever been so frustrated, upset, broken or that emotionally wrecked. I have so much respect for people with a disability of any sort, be it like my story or worse. It was so incredibly hard for me not to get annoyed about the fact I couldn't get anyone to understand me, I was convinced I was dying. I was constantly thinking I was going to die within the next few minutes. It is the ONLY time I have ever thought about death, about my own death. I didn't want to die, I was scared; so scared.

Although I couldn't concentrate on anything going on around me, I still remember to this day when I was lying in that hospital bed in the ICU, thinking about my funeral, what it would be like to die and not exist anymore. I was so scared and couldn't quite understand why I was alive when everything had been taken away from me. Of course, at the time I had no idea that I had actually died and been brought back to life a few times and that my family were all told to prepare for the worst. I only found that out a few years ago. When I found this out, I think I went to my room and cried because it suddenly hit me and loads of memories came flooding back in, these were either things that I had forgotten or just simply wasn't aware of, but now it all made sense. I died. I died and was brought back to life, that empty, lonely place where I felt I didn't belong for me must've been where I went when I was on my way out of this world, though it wasn't my time to go.

I remember my brother Ricki visiting me and I wanted to ask him loads of questions, make fun of him, wind him up; but all I could do was lie there completely useless and almost lifeless just staring at him.

Angel bought me a PSP (PlayStation Portable). She got me a

few films and games that I could hopefully try and play later on, once recovery began. At this time, she put on movies and sat and held it there for us to watch. I was very easily agitated, very easily upset, unable to communicate, I was a mess. I couldn't concentrate even 5 minutes into the film, I was fed up that I couldn't sit up, or that I couldn't even simply roll onto my side, the little everyday things that most people take for granted, do you? I did. I sure as hell now try my best to be as positive as I can. This isn't always the case, but I will always reflect to these moments and realise how much I have overcome.

Angel and BFATT had bought me King Kong, The Office, Wedding Crashers, The Mighty Boosh and Lemmings. I remember being angry, for no other reason than not wanting to be in that hospital bed. I remember looking at 'King Kong' and not having anything run through my head, I was empty, completely empty. I didn't have a clue what was going on. I often got upset, angry or frustrated for no reason. I couldn't work out the emotions that I was going through, they all became one emotion. One big emotional ball of mess. Even though I remember being angry and frustrated I cannot deny the excitement I felt but couldn't express when Angel and BFATT told me and showed me the PSP. I thought *how cool!!* Then the realisation that I was unable to use it, hit me. As time went on my concentration did get better, but not by much and my emotions were the same. My emotions were flat for quite some time.

Looking back and thinking about the chemo treatment and how I felt going through cancer compared to the stroke are a completely different batch of emotions. During cancer treatment I was able to communicate, able to see people and able to move about. Even if that meant I needed help to get up and about due to feeling weak from the chemo I was independent, to a certain extent. When the stroke hit, when I finally realised what was going on. I hated it. I hated feeling that low, that weak and that useless. To be completely unable to communicate, unable to smile, laugh, cry, eat, drink, sit up. Unable to do anything for myself, I was broken. I was scared and I was broken. I only wanted my family & BFATT near me. I didn't want anyone else to see me, I didn't want to see me. I didn't feel like me. I wanted the world to stop picking on me and making me battle. I thought I had won the fight.

Sigh.

The fight has just begun all over again.

CHAPTER 10

INTENSIVE CARE

The Intensive Care Unit (ICU).

Ah. So that's where I am?

I remember thinking that to myself quite a few times. Then I'd forget, be reminded by a nurse or by my family and then I'd forget, again.
Before anyone was even allowed to step foot into my room, they had to wash their hands thoroughly, wear aprons, wear disposable plastic shoe covers, and they also had to wear gloves; this was highly important amongst this entire unit. Due to the nature of the patients within the ICU, everyone was in a bad place. Not that I could see any other patients, which I was very glad for because hell, if this was how crap I was feeling, I sure as hell didn't want to see what others looked like.
I also had never been so grateful in my life NOT to see a mirror. Now if you know me, you'll know I'm not very vain, or at least I don't think I am. I took a VERY long time to ever want to look at myself in the mirror again following on

from the stroke. I just didn't feel me at all, I don't know what I felt; but I knew I didn't want to see myself.
Looking at myself during cancer treatment was hard, with the hair loss, looking frail and fragile; but boy oh boy looking at yourself in a mirror after a stroke, no. Just. No.
I would say even to this day it is something that I still struggle with, yup 17 years on. It was very hard not only adjusting to life with cancer and people seeing me differently and the look, oh that look. The look a stranger gives you after a stroke, is beyond describable. It's a look where you wish so hard that the ground will swallow you up and help you disappear. This was to come much later though; I hadn't seen what I looked like yet and to be honest my attention span was about 2 seconds.

Sorry? Ah yes. I'm in The Intensive Care Unit. I would thank you for repeating yourself for the fiftieth time in an hour, however...I can't speak.

Hang on.

Wait.

Will I ever speak again?

Shit. Those are my legs?

I can't move.

Will I stand again?

Hang on, what's walking?

With all of that constantly going through my head it was emotionally draining. Also, very frustrating not being able to speak, and not being heard. Of course, it wasn't just hard and upsetting for me. My family and BFATT also must have struggled as they were unable to speak for me or know what I was thinking. It was frustrating for all of us. I was so sad at this point, so unlike me. I remained as positive as I could during the battle with cancer, which was still not over yet. I still needed to hit that 5-year mark to be in complete remission. At this point in time during the stroke, in my head I thought cancer was hard. *OH, THIS isn't a side effect of chemo? THIS is something NEW? A stroke!? A STROKE!? I'm only 18. Only older people are at risk of strokes?* All these questions, yet I couldn't ask a single one. I was still unable to talk. I was confused by the fact I couldn't speak. I didn't understand.

Having my family and BFATT visit was difficult as it must have been hard for them to see me in that state, I appreciated seeing them every day. So, thank you. Thank you, Mum, Dad, Angel, Vicky, Ricki, BFATT. Thank you to BFATT's Mum who I believe made my family her infamous carrot cake. She came to visit me; she held my hand so tight. I don't remember if you said anything but thank you for being supportive to my family and then for continuing your support to myself over the 8 years that I was with BFATT. BFATT's parents L & B, thank you.

To my friends who weren't sure of what was going on with me at the time as it was so 'touch and go' it was limited as to what you may have been told, I remember closing my eyes to say "no" when I was asked if I wanted anyone else visiting. I won't apologise for that, because I know it would've broken me for any of you to have seen me in that state, I still was yet to see myself. I don't fully understand the difficulties you guys may have gone through to piece together what was going on with me. I hope these pages paint a better picture so that you are able to piece it together yourselves, if you haven't already.

Thank you for still being there today, and for ALWAYS being there for me. I love you guys. Now and always.
There are hundreds of people I have to thank; I haven't forgotten you. If you haven't been mentioned yet but are in my life, I do care about you. There were so many amazing people, friends, friends of friends and family. In fact, people that I didn't even really know. A ton of you during my treatments for cancer, stroke, before cancer, before the stroke, and after all this crazy. People that I care about. If you are in my life, thank you.
Now, where was I? Yes, Intensive care! So, as you can imagine there is a lot to talk about during this and a lot to cover.
Amongst the craziness of me, my family & BFATT making up our own sign language, me pooping myself every few hours and not being able to join in any conversations, I realised this was not going to be an easy ride. This was going to suck, and I already hated it. I didn't think I'd ever get to where I am today and I have the NHS staff to thank for that and every single person that cared for me during the ten months in hospital, and the many years after. Most importantly my family, friends & BFATT too as without the support of them, I would NEVER have smiled again. I didn't see the point; I was dying anyway, right?

WRONG.

I wrote on a notepad to BFATT once, in a red felt tip pen "Die?" It took about 8 minutes to write, no exaggeration there. It may have even taken longer. BFATT tore the page and stormed out. I couldn't turn to see where he'd gone or call after him. Seconds later Angel (possibly my Mum, bit hazy here) came into the room. She explained to me for the hundredth time that I wasn't dying. She's a tough cookie, a hard one to break. I have only seen her cry like twice in my lifetime, yet I could see the tears she fought back in her eyes.

Looking back, I think I was trying to ask if I was dying, maybe part of me thought it would be easier to die as I felt everyone was fighting so hard to keep me alive. Everyone but me. I will never forget the look Angel gave me that day. BFATT came back in, and they said I'm not allowed to think like that anymore or write anything like that again. I don't believe I ever did again, but I still had those thoughts. They were less often as time went on. This feeling of death I had and thinking it was easier to die, was me giving up. I really didn't think I would survive this; I didn't think I would ever leave that room and I thought I would die in that bed. The positivity I had through my chemotherapy had been completely sucked out of me, I was feeling low; I had lost hope in myself. I remember this one day when BFATT and Angel came to visit. I say came to visit…I'll just paint a picture to you guys - all my family stayed cramped in a tiny room around the corner from where I was in the ICU, just so they could be with me 24/7. They took it in turns to come and see me, swapping who would stay and who would go home or to work. They had some sort of rota amongst themselves.

Angel, I believe you gave up your job to be with me – I love you, and I thank you like you would not believe. Thank you for leaving your home behind to be at my side in Bristol. The rest of you, thank you for fitting me into your lives whilst also trying to maintain your own.

I heard a rustling, like tissue paper. I saw a gift bag with two things wrapped in tissue paper. They had presents! They had to open the gift for me as I couldn't, it was a dog collar and a small dog bowl! Now, out of context this sounds random, these weren't gifts for me. Let's rewind to the first memory I have after the stroke. Seeing my Mum and Dad. Seeing them torn apart all over again, but this time; it was worse. "You need to get through this Leena, you got through cancer, stay with us. I promise you if you pull through this you will get the dog you have always wanted. We will get you a dog. Stay with us."

I didn't want to die, my fear when I was first diagnosed with cancer was thinking I might die. Turns out it was the stroke that did it, but I was luckily enough brought back and slowly building up within myself to fight. To fight again. Since I was young, I always dreamt of having a dog, then throughout cancer I thought it'd be so lush to have one. However, as I was in and out of hospitals so much and needed to be away from germs we wouldn't have been home, or able to walk a dog. I remember thinking *I can get through this,* then seconds later thinking *nope. It's too hard.*

I was so excited when they showed me the gifts, I remember wanting to ask where the dog was.

Clearly, I was confused, and my brain was struggling to piece things together, after a while I think I understood. I was excited, but it would be a long time until I was better and perhaps an even longer time until I could have a dog, one day I hoped, one day.

As I became stronger in myself, they started introducing the care team into my room to begin rehabilitation. It took a while before I reached this stage. Before this point there were endless days of feeling low, endless days of not knowing if I was going to get better. Sleepless nights for everyone. They introduced me to a speech therapist, whose name I have forgotten and a physiotherapy team to help me learn to walk again, I'm not sure which came first. I do however remember when I was first learning to stand with numerous staff around me, once I stood up with the support of many nurses...things left my body. Yes, it was disgusting, pooing myself again, great. I was so upset, I looked to my sister Angel for help. I had so many people trying to clean me whilst also trying to keep me standing. *Nope. I'm done*, I thought. *Put me back in that bed please.* I have never felt so upset and so void. I was broken. This really and I mean really, sucked.

Please clean me, I still feel dirty, I thought. *Please don't look at me*

I'm embarrassed, I thought.

I want to cry, I can't.

I want to talk to you, but I can't.

I want to scream, I can't.

I want to go home.

I can't.

Over the next few weeks, the care teams came to me again to try and help me stand up. I refused a few times, now I don't remember how long it took me to get over the poo-nami but I was mentally scarred by it. I didn't want them to come back again. I couldn't even tell anyone how sorry I was that it happened, neither was I able to warn anyone it was about to happen because I didn't know when I needed to go. Eventually over a longgggg time, the feeling of needing to go came back, and I would show whoever was in the room two fingers for a 'number 2' or just point down. They got the gist. Anyway, shall we move on from my bowel movements? This part of my journey wasn't pleasant; there were so many things over the duration of the 10 months of me being in hospital that made me feel low and embarrassed, of course it was out of my control but feeling low during these moments was very apparent.
The Speech Therapist lady was lovely, although when she first came in, I turned my head the opposite way to her. I was angry that she could speak and that I was unable to.

Where is my voice?

After my family spoke to me, to tell me that she was there to help me, and I needed to try and let her help me. I realised I need to work for all the things that I had lost. Things that were taken from me over a few moments, overnight. I now have to spend the rest of my life to get better. I need to work at getting back something that was taken from me, the ability to walk again, the ability to talk again, the ability to eat and drink, the ability to live again. No one can do it, but me?

I can do this.

I can.

Can I?

As I cannot remember the Speech Therapist's name, we'll call her "ST" for short.
Firstly, ST got me to do a simple nod after each question, a nod to you is easy right? I see you nodding! There we go. Well for me, a nod took ages, a whole 2 minutes, yes. This is a long time, because I said the word nod you would've instantly done that, without even thinking twice. These messages weren't getting sent to my brain, so the little things took a very long time.

ST: Do you have two sisters?

Me: …...........................Nod

ST: Are they called Angel & Vicky?

Me:…...

Me:….....

Me: ….................Nod

ST: Do you have a brother called Ricki?

Me:….................

Me:…................................Nod

I remember the relief in the early days after the stroke that I was able to recognise my family and BFATT. The medical care team were overwhelmed with joy, as this meant my memory of who they were was unaffected. I am very lucky that none of my memories have gone, I treasure every single one. The good and the bad.
After she asked these questions, I felt tired. ST could see that I was tired and said that was enough for now, but she would be back tomorrow. Over the next few days, she tried new exercises with me. She brought in this weird machine which spoke out what you typed in. I HATED IT. I HATED IT. I HATED IT!

I want to talk, but a machine is doing it for me.

NO.

NO, THANK YOU.

ST could tell I wasn't a fan of this device as I turned my head away from her. I recall Angel telling ST that it was upsetting me, and as they were unable to know why I was upset they needed to try other ways.
They tried with this stupid machine a few more times over the next few sessions.
However, they could see it was breaking me, so they moved it out of sight eventually. Looking back, I remember being angry because the machine sounded robotic, and it made me feel so little. Little because a tiny handheld device in its robotic tone was able to communicate, but I was unable to. I wanted to grab it and throw it out of the window, but I was unable to use my arms and hands, so I just sulked in silence. I was broken.
ST had a few exercises to help build back the muscles in my face, to retrain my brain I needed to make these movements to form my mouth in different ways, to then make a sound. This was all very tiring and confusing.

Where is my voice?

Hours passed; days went on. *Has my voice gone forever?*

More hours passed; even more days went on…

"One"

HOLY CRAP did I just say something!?

"One"

OH MY GOD THIS IS ME!!! I am talking!!

“One”

I DON'T RECOGNISE THIS VOICE, BUT I THINK IT'S MINE!?

"One"

WHY DO I KEEP SAYING THE NUMBER ONE

“One”

ST was getting me to try and count to 5. It took me days of trying to move my mouth, endless emotional moments of frustration when I just couldn’t. I couldn’t do it. I wished she would stop talking at me.

“One”

HOLLLLLLLY MOLY I SAID SOMETHING

“ONE”

The first word I EVER said after the stroke was “One”. I said it over and over. My brain liked this word, my brain only knew this word. *I can say “one” now,* I thought to myself. *Let’s get to two!!!*

ST: How are you feeling today, Leena?

Me: ......One

Oh.

This might take longer than I realise.

CHAPTER 11

ONCOLOGY

"One."

ST was so passionate about her job and very caring. She had kind eyes, a soft but authoritative voice and I warmed to her. I especially liked her because she was the reason, I could finally say a word and make a sound. The word "one."

Even if it didn't sound like my voice, I knew it came from me and that was a good sign. It was tiring to say this small, simple word a handful of times. We just don't know how lucky we are guys, never take the smallest things for granted. When we want to speak (if we can) we just simply speak, there is no thought process other than knowing we are about to speak and what we want to say. Our brain is so incredible at knowing what we want to say or do before we do these simple tasks, yet we don't appreciate how incredible it is to open our mouths and say words; we just say them.

After a brain injury it is so much more than that, you have to tell your brain that you want to speak, but your brain has forgotten what that function is and how to switch it back on. It isn't aware that you were even able to speak before, your brain is trying to rewire and heal but you have to put this

effort in to help your brain, it cannot work alone. This was hard to comprehend during this time because I didn't have a clue what was going on or why my brain was giving up.
Over the next few days, ST continued with counting, and encouraging me to get to the number 5.

ST: What comes after the number one Leena?

Me: One

ST: Nope, it goes one, two...

Me: One, one...

ST: You can say one now which is amazing but try and start with the number two. You can do it; I know you can.

Me: T, T, T...one

This went on for a very hard and tiring amount of time over the next few days. I knew in my head that the number two came after one, but my brain wasn't sending that message to my mouth. Therefore one, two, three became one, one, one for quite some time. A very long time. An annoyingly long time. I thought that perhaps this was going to be my only way of communicating for the rest of my life, just with one word. The word 'one.' This alone was a lot for me to take in, the fact that it was so exhausting to say one single word and to make the smallest sound.

Is this my life now?

Am I stuck like this forever?

As a break to counting and to not put too much stress on me, ST tried a new exercise. Smiling. Trying to get those muscles in my face going again. Someone in my family had got me a mirror so that I could see myself whilst we were trying the exercises. ST had mentioned that it would be good for in between her visits for me to continue with the exercises and having a mirror would help me see my progress.

Who is that in the reflection?

She looks awful.

Why is her face lopsided and drooping so much?

Why is she dribbling?

Why are you showing me that person?

Wait. Does she know she's dribbling?

She looks confused and there is sadness in her eyes.

Wait.

Is that

Is that me?

That's me. I look awful. My face is drooping on one side, I'm drooling like a dog, and I don't like the way I look. I don't recognise myself.

I wondered how long I had been dribbling for, probably this entire time as I couldn't feel my face and had no idea this giant dribble was travelling down my neck.

I'm done. I quit.

I will never fully be able to describe to you that feeling of when I first saw myself in the mirror after the stroke, but I will try. After a few moments I shut my eyes, then reopened them as if it was some sort of bad dream. However, the same sad reflection stared back at me. It was a feeling of sorrow, I didn't just feel sorry for myself, but I felt sorry for whatever that person in the reflection was going through. Realising again, that yup, that person was me. It tore me apart, I felt confused all over again. I knew I wasn't in a good place, but I didn't like the way I looked, that person couldn't be me. She looked void, distant, ill. She was me. That dribbling mess was me.

ST could tell that seeing my reflection was upsetting me and, as she was unable to work out what was wrong, she looked at the sorrow in my eyes and lowered the mirror. I could just about handle only seeing my mouth, which again was drooping on the right side. It was still hard to see that small part of my face, but it was so much easier not to see the rest. These exercises were ongoing for the next few weeks. The feeling of not liking what I saw in the mirror went on for the next few months, to a few years. I'm not talking about not liking the reflection because I disliked my body shape or thought I was too fat or too thin, I mean I disliked the reflection looking back at me because I simply did not recognise myself anymore, I felt broken because the stroke had affected more than just my brain; it affected everything. It felt like I would never be me again and that I would be stuck with this void and emptiness forever.

Amongst trying to learn to speak again and learning to sit up with help, was also the need to be able to eat, chew and swallow because this feeding tube needed to go! I needed to work hard for that to happen, and it didn't sound like it was going to be a quick fix, none of this was. Before I would be able to leave the ICU, I needed to be able to do some basic things that we all perhaps take for granted. I needed to be able to chew food so that it broke down enough and enabled me to be able to swallow whatever food I was eating. I also

needed to be able to drink, however easy it is to say I needed to do these things, my brain had switched off and I didn't even know what these things meant at the time. I didn't have my brain telling my body to do a simple task such as chewing or swallowing a drink. To start training my brain again, they needed to see what function of my throat was in place. The nurses started by soaking small sponges in water to see if I was able to suck any of the water out. I choked. I choked, machines beeped, I choked again, I gasped for air. After this attempt they left it for another day as it was a little bit traumatic. Who knew that so much information was required to hit your brain to then enable you to pick up a drink and take a sip? It's just a simple day to day task that we all do and perhaps never give a second thought. We just do it right?
Be grateful that you just do these things, because when it gets taken away, and I sure as hell hope none of you ever have to go through this; but when it gets taken away from you it's very hard to get that back. It took me weeks of sucking water out of a sponge until I was able to swallow it and stop choking.

My brain was slowly, and I mean SLOWLY starting to re-wire.

S L O W L Y.

The feeding tube needed to stay in a bit longer as I was unable to chew food or drink more than a few sips of water without choking. Sips of water, through a tiny piece of sponge. It was a sponge on the end of a stick, I guess they usually use those to soak up blood whilst a patient was in surgery. I highly doubt they were designed for a stroke patient to suck liquids through; however, I was very grateful that a nurse came up with the idea as throughout all the choking it was nice to do something that was deemed 'normal' even though me and my little brain felt like this was

a new thing that we had just learnt for the very first time.
After a very, VERY long time of feeling like I was closer to death each day within the intensive care unit, there were talks of me potentially going back to Ward 62 in the Oncology department. That feeling of thinking I was dying is the worst I have ever felt in my life, and I hope I never feel like that again. Each moment of a new day I felt closer to death than I did to recovery, this isn't an exaggeration or a cry for your sympathy this is just me telling it how it was and quite bluntly. I did not want to die, but there were moments where I felt like dying would perhaps be easier than keeping me alive. These are thoughts I had at the time and luckily have never crossed my mind since, what a horrible place and mindset to be in. There is no way to paint a pretty picture here because it just wasn't the case.
The nurses and doctors were discussing with my family about moving me back to Ward 62 - remember, this is where I had been before, up until the stroke happened. I think Dr Evely was the one that came to tell me that I was doing well, this was good news. As it meant I was no longer critical and in need of Intensive Care. Dr Evely came to see how I was doing a few times; I'll never forget the first time I saw him. I squeezed his hand so tight, '*help me*' I thought. This man was an absolute hero to me and my family, we will forever adore you and your team for keeping me alive.

I was in the ICU ward for several weeks, I'm not too sure how long it was, but it was tough. This wasn't an easy ride, I didn't wake up in intensive care after having a stroke and miraculously recover in a few days to walk out of there, that just isn't reality. Life just doesn't work like that, life is hard, and life is a gamble BUT I am a true believer in hope, where there is hope there will be a smile again. Even if I needed to smile through dribble, you will see this one smile again. I was not positive at all during my time in the ICU; there were moments I felt okay but not many. If I am completely honest with you guys, I don't think I was positive for a very long time during this period of my story. I had good days and bad days with the chemo, with the stroke there were so many bad days it is hard to remember the good. What I do know is that those around me, even through all this, remained positive, they fought for me...so boy oh boy did I have some fighting to do too.

I will never fully be able to find the words that could even begin to describe this part of my life to you. For my family to have a phone call to tell them that I was in a bad way, and that they had to prepare for the worst is something no family should ever have to hear. To be told that they needed to come back to the hospital and say bye to me is only something that I found out a few years after the stroke.

I am very lucky I had the patience of the NHS staff, my family, BFATT and my friends because I kid you not recovery does not come overnight. I wished it did, every birthday for the next few years this was my wish when I blew out those candles. I just wanted everything back that was taken away.

Now people say you shouldn't ever mention your wish as it won't come true. Even though I have not fully recovered today, I am sitting here writing this and I guess it came true in its own way. I am well and I can share these stories with you, even if it means I need to type the majority of this one handed. My right-hand joins in when it can and when I remember to tell my brain that it still has two arms and hands.

HEY BRAIN WE GOT THIS!

It is the toughest thing I have ever had to go through. Don't get me wrong, cancer was hard, but there was a drug for that, Chemo, Chemo was my friend. Cancer was tough, but the stroke - give me strength. There is nothing to cure a stroke. You may never fully recover from one and I was without a doubt incredibly lucky to have even survived it, I was in the

worst possible way.
If I could give you a glimpse of the pain, emotion, and destruction it caused to my life and those around me - I wouldn't.
When I was diagnosed with cancer, I briefly thought *why me?* Then I realised that I was so grateful it wasn't my family or friends lying in that bed. Everything was taken away from me when that stroke hit, it took everything. It did not however take away the love and care from my family, friends and BFATT.
Once the ICU team battled to keep me alive, it was then a constant battle to stay alive. My family were told that even if I did survive this that I may not be the same. They could not promise or guarantee anything in terms of my recovery, and if I would be able to recover at all. There was a chance that my memory of who they all were might not be there, my memories may have been void of all time, my speech may never return, and I may never walk again. I only found out all of this a few years after the stroke, once I was stable enough to handle that type of information. I do remember hearing the words "she may never walk again" whilst I was in the ICU. I just shut down after hearing that. I shut down a lot of times.
It must have been November 2006 by the time I was moved from the ICU back to Oncology, and it felt so nice to be within familiar grounds and within a room that wasn't surrounded by tons of medical equipment. I felt happier here, but also broken. All the staff that treated me for cancer came in to see me. I gave the smallest smile ever when I saw them, as it was all I was able to do, it was more of a twitch than a smile; but it was something.
I was still not able to fully communicate. I believe I could only count to three at this point, which everyone was excited by. I still said the word "one" several times throughout the day. I was also able to shake my head and nod.
Physiotherapy sessions did begin in the ICU, however as

there was so much medical equipment surrounding me and as I needed so much to keep me alive it was limited as to how much I was able to do.
So, within the ICU it was heavily focused on my Speech Therapy, which is where the hard work began.
My physiotherapist was called Jos, he was so so SO patient with me, and I was an awful patient. In fact, it could not have been more opposite than the word.
Suffering from a stroke sends your emotions into a crazy whirlwind above you and follows you around for what seems like forever. When I first saw him, I was confused about why he wanted me to walk. I remember thinking *he knows I can't walk right?*

Then I remember thinking, *crap. I have to learn to walk again?*

This was taken from me in seconds, can it not just be given back to me in a few moments?

No?

Fine.

All of this was tough, tough on me and tough on those around me. Being back on Ward 62 meant that anyone could stay with me, my Mum and Dad were there throughout the days and my family & BFATT staggered visits between work and their lives.
My Mum could tell I didn't want to try and walk on this one particular day, but Jos and my Mum insisted that I tried, even if it was just to sit up in bed. I sulked. This repeated over the next few days. Then one day Jos said he was not leaving until I at least tried to walk to the doorway. I guess a big part of me was scared that I would poo myself again, also my brain didn't understand whose legs they were either, I feared my own body. Scared because I was unable to control any of it

or recognise it as my own. With the help of Jos and a few others in the physio team I was able to stand and I'm pretty sure my body was being dragged as opposed to me holding myself up, but it felt so good to not be lying down in that hospital bed even if I did have numerous staff holding me up over the next few days.

These physio sessions continued, instead of spending the whole day in my hospital gown or in my pyjamas they had mentioned to Mum that I should get a routine going, wake up and get ready for the day – even if I wasn't going anywhere. To me this seemed odd if I'm not going anywhere what's the point?

Wrong.

Getting up and getting ready for the day EVEN if you are not going somewhere 100% makes a difference to your state of mind. It helped me so much then, and it helps me so much now. Of course, don't get me wrong, if I want a rest day and to sit in lounge wear all day watching Netflix I can and I will, however this is about balance and it's a treat for me to do that. I have learned to do this more often and take days to myself because actually even now I struggle with consistently doing something and I have learned to balance things a lot better.

I needed help getting dressed, getting showered, basically everything. Like the days when I was weak from all the chemo, I needed help, again. I hated the fact I was unable to do all these simple tasks by myself. I was really upset, I wondered how long I would need help with the day-to-day tasks, and I wondered if this was my life now. Needing care 24/7. I missed everything, I missed being able to sit up, brush my own teeth, shower myself, dry myself, dress myself, hold a knife and fork, cut my own food, feed myself, look in the mirror and not cry. I missed my band Incured, I missed playing gigs, I missed playing the drums, I missed everything that I took for granted as an 18-year-old. I missed my life; I missed me.

The nurses were amazing. My Mum offered to help them bathe me at times as I needed support, they let her as I was so upset that so many people needed to do this task for me. It felt so demeaning having to have others wash me. I of course was unable to move or do any of this myself for a long time, so this feeling, unfortunately, lasted for a very long time.

Gradually, after even more endless days my "good arm" (the left arm) became stronger; it now needed to become my dominant side as my right side was completely shut off. For now. I was able to brush my teeth for a few seconds a day whilst my Mum helped me when my left hand got tired. I was able to stand for a few more seconds longer, with help. I took a few more steps each day. My emotions went from sad, happy, angry, depressed, annoyed, okay, and upset within seconds of each other.

This time spent on Oncology was spent trying to get my life back on track, and no one knew how many years it would take. Not months, years. I am still recovering. If I'm tired, you may notice I slur my words. If I get excited and speak too fast none of the words even sound like words. Sometimes I'll be misheard, and I won't repeat what I have said, because I close up and remember what it was like in the early days when no one understood a single thing I said. I felt like an alien every time I opened my mouth, like I was speaking some unheard-of language, not English.

Certain sounds I still cannot make or articulate, or it just takes me a little bit longer than most to say.

For example, if I wanted to say "Thor" it sounded like "Four" etc etc.

I found it extremely hard once I got my voice back to then **want to be heard**. I was constantly misunderstood, so then I spoke quieter. To lose your voice and not be heard is one thing. Then to have your voice back and want to be heard and understood is even harder. I hated speaking in the early days of recovery, it didn't sound like me. It was frustrating to not be understood by those close to me. Then as years went on, even now for certain words not to be understood or if I slur and you notice it, it is hard for me to want to repeat myself again or talk in a hurry. I wasn't sure if I wanted to mention this part in the book, but I feel it's important, it's important to me and I want it to be important for you to understand that we don't always understand anyone else's journey in life, I don't know everything or anything about you, the same way that you don't know everything about me. Unless of course you're reading this book then you'll know a fair bit about me by this point…

Having a speech impairment is tough, it is very subtle to me...however at times I still notice it and it can upset me if I am misunderstood. I usually try my best to make it into a joke and laugh through it rather than cry. This doesn't mean I'm unaffected by how you've reacted, it just means I'm trying to find a way to deal with your response. This is just how I am now, and you'll just have to understand; that's on you, be patient and caring please. Crying happens SO much, the stroke played havoc on my emotions, so when I can have a laugh and joke about things I will, I will always choose laughter over tears. Unless it's crying with laughter, that's the best.

Now I'm not having a go at you if in the past you have ever asked me to repeat what I have just said, or if you didn't understand a word or if you've laughed at me for mispronouncing something. I'm simply saying, hey, here's my story, therefore these things may have happened.

It is something I found really hard to deal with at the age of 18. It knocked all confidence I ever had, and I just felt low. Slurred speech, dribbling when I was trying to learn to speak again and then over the years of recovery and even now, I still find this element of recovery tough; BUT I don't want your sympathy I just want you to understand that recovery after a stroke is not easy. None of this was or is easy. It isn't an overnight fix and for many sometimes there isn't a fix at all.

If you are reading this and there are certain elements of your life where you may have gone through something like me, it is okay to feel low. We are all human and we are allowed to have an 'off' day. You just need to make sure you can pick yourself back up again, even if it means that others literally have to pick you up. I spent a lot of time trying to stand up and my legs would just go to jelly.

I shut myself off to a lot of you from November 2006 for around 2 years, maybe longer, maybe less. I was in a place where I didn't want to know anyone outside of my family circle and BFATT. I didn't want anyone to view or judge me differently, as I didn't feel like I was the person they knew anymore. I wasn't Leena. I was unable to text anyone as my movement was limited or non-existent, the same with social media, I was unable to type or too annoyed to see everyone out having fun and living their lives, when I was unable to do the same. We had Myspace back when I was 18, oh how things have changed! I used to change the coding and have a little dancing Borat in the corner. Oh, the simpler times.

It took me a long time to find myself again, to build the smallest bits of confidence back each day. It took years of patience from my family, BFATT, friends, NHS staff and even more years to get myself to a better place. I am very lucky that I was surrounded by someone everyday even when I felt low, their presence just made me feel slightly better, even if by the smallest amount.

The reason I said earlier that I don't want any sympathy is because I felt so sorry for myself, for a very long time. Feeling sorry for myself got me nowhere. Feeling low and bottling all these emotions up got me nowhere, they just delayed my progress and made each day even harder to want to wake up. Thank you to everyone who kept me going, even when I wanted to quit so often. Thank you for holding me up until

I was able to stand again. Thank you for always standing by my side.
I urge you all to try and be more open, even if you don't want to. I am very lucky that my family, BFATT and that my friends never gave up on me. I am very lucky to have the most incredible people in my life that never judged me, even when I judged myself so badly.

Remember that notepad I spoke about earlier on?

Well, I FOUND IT.

I have no idea what I was trying to write here. I do know that it is one of the first things I tried to write with my left hand, the only limb that I was able to move. My brain was still in the early stages of recovery and just about clinging onto the fact it was in control of my limbs. My left arm and hand really struggled after the stroke, and I remember how exhausted I felt after writing this. I also remember feeling so frustrated in that moment because no one understood what I wrote. At the time this would have meant something to my brain and to me, looking at it now there is no way this would have made sense to anyone…it doesn't even make sense to me now, but I wrote it and that was progress!

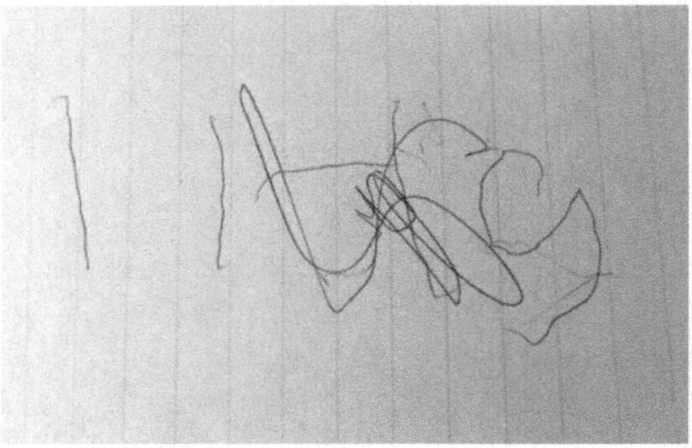

WAHOO! A full sentence, however, it took me so long to write this. I'm sure I pooed myself whilst writing it.

Give me the PSP! When I started feeling stronger and when Angel and BFATT entered my room, this is often what I would write. Even though I couldn't hold the PSP myself and they often had to play it for me or place my hands on it, so it felt like I was playing. I really believe this helped my recovery. Seeing something familiar felt really comforting, and I really loved game consoles at the time…I still do I just can't really hold a controller for long, they aren't really designed well for someone with disabilities like mine, but it doesn't mean I won't try.

Angel wrote these out for me whilst I was in the ICU and we used them when I was back on the Oncology ward too. I was unable to speak or communicate, when my left hand got stronger, I was able to point to the words in the pad so everyone knew how I was feeling or if I was in any pain; not that I could feel anything yet.

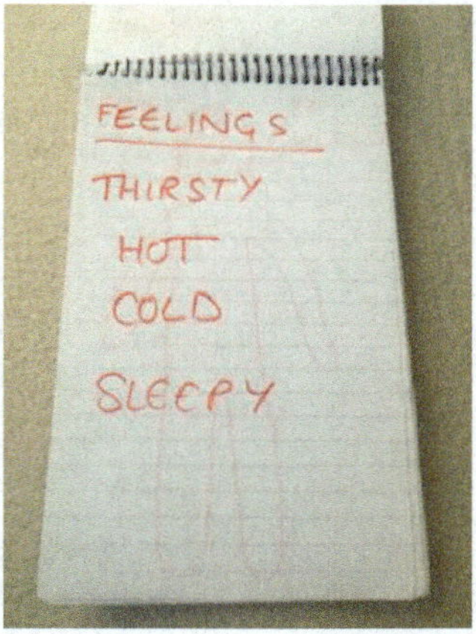

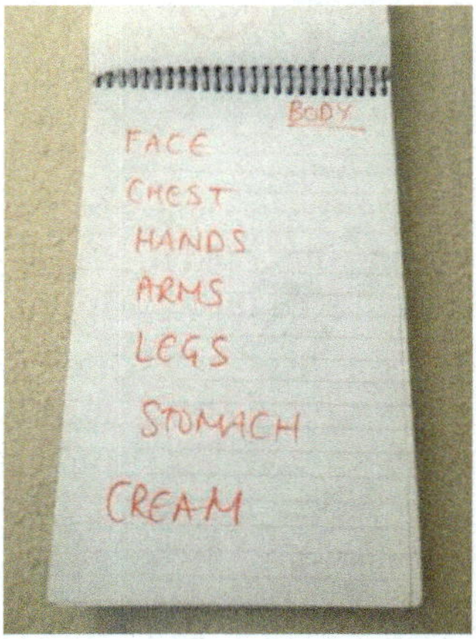

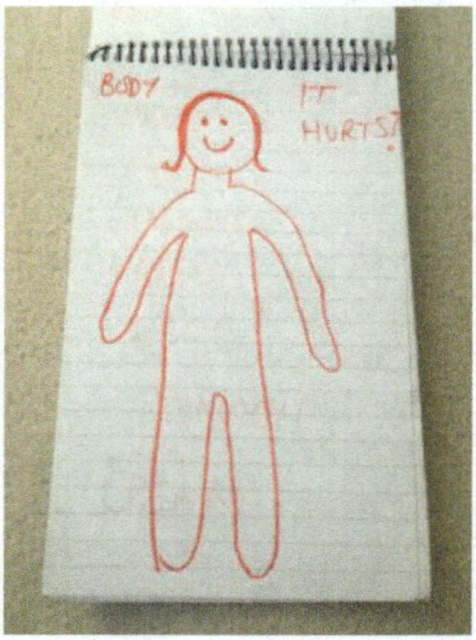

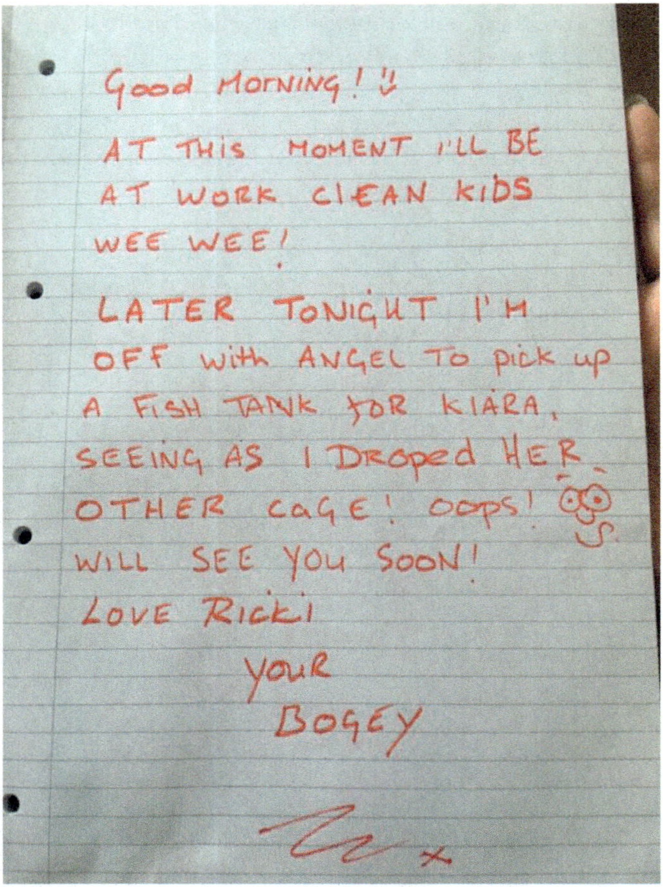
Good Morning!
AT THIS MOMENT I'LL BE AT WORK CLEAN KIDS WEE WEE!
LATER TONIGHT I'M OFF with ANGEL TO pick up A FISH TANK FOR KIARA, SEEING AS I DROPED HER OTHER cage! oops!
WILL SEE YOU SOON!
Love Ricki
your Bogey
x

My siblings and BFATT always left messages or notes if I was asleep. Then the next person visiting me could then read them to me if I had missed their visit. I loved this, I may not have been able to react at the time, but I thank you guys for doing this for me, it was the best. I must add here that my brother doesn't eat his bogeys or anything gross like that, but growing up as siblings do, we always picked on each other and he hated that I called him bogey once. So, I carried on calling him that for many, many years. Another note is that

Kiara was a pet hamster, I'm not sure if he dropped her cage with her in it...maybe my parents ought to rethink us ever having a dog that they promised me, eh?
Now I don't remember much, but I remember thinking, does Ricki know what a chore is? Haha, kidding bro. The house was still standing when I eventually made it home so that was a good sign. Whilst I was in ICU, I gradually had enough strength in my left hand to give a thumbs up. A lot of the time it was thumbs down, but as the days went on the thumbs down were outweighed by the thumbs up.

Angel - this made me smile then and it still makes me smile now.

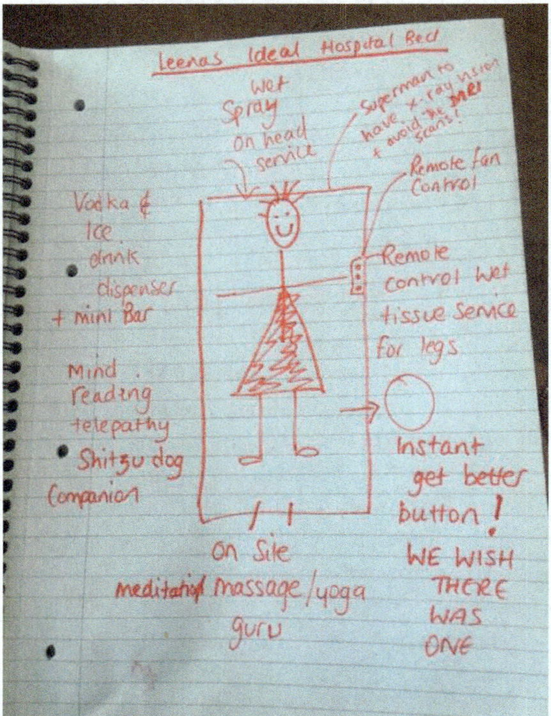

CHAPTER 12

DRAW A CLOCK

Before this book came to be I started this process off as blog posts during Lockdown 2020. I needed a way to kickstart the creative process; and with all the time we had with Covid-19 and its impact on the world it was the perfect setting for me to write. I started writing this book at the age of 22 but the blog posts have been within the past few years, and this is now the book I dreamt I would finally complete, so I do hope you are enjoying it.

My sister Angel texted me after reading a blog post that I put online over lockdown and said that when I was in ICU it was critical care, hour by hour as to whether or not I would make it through. I had samples of blood couriered off to London for a full screening to see if I had meningitis. I found out after coming across my hospital things that I suffered from 'Post Infective Encephalitis' on the 6th November 2006. This is a virus/infection that attacks the immune system, which then led on to inflammation in my brain, which then led onto the stroke.

I believe this journey of mine would take years to fully describe, years may not even cover it. There is so much emotion and distress that comes with cancer and a stroke, but I am so happy that I get to sit here and tell you my story, to share with you something so important to me, the things that shaped who I am today.

The speech therapy continued as did the physiotherapy sessions. I became more and more stronger as the days went on, my patience was at an all-time low and I really struggled throughout the days and into the next. At this point I still had the feeding tube in, I was able to drink without choking now although the muscles in my face and throat still weren't strong enough for me to be able to eat yet.

As this ward was devoted to the care of cancer patients, the doctors were having meetings about my next steps and where I might need to go to carry on with the rehabilitation. All I could think was how much I missed my own bed, that I really wanted to home but also battling with the thought that I was not well enough to, I was still trying to piece it all together. I was starting to forget what my own room looked like and how much longer it might be before I ever made it back home, hospitals became my home for the majority of 2006, and then some. It took absolutely AGES to get to this next part of my journey that I am about to share with you, but it was such a good day and I felt so proud and so relieved with something so small, something that we just don't think about day to day. That something I tell you now, was walking up the SMALLEST flight of stairs, perhaps 6 steps, but with the **least** amount of help I required in my recovery to date. I CANNOT express to you the sheer amount of joy that these few steps brought to my life. I remember thinking in my head during each step *"she might not ever walk again"*, watch me.

It took a lot of concentration and energy, also a lot of patience from Jos and my Mum. Jos thought in order to get me to push myself a little bit further than my bed to the doorway, that he needed to think of targets and things I needed to reach. So, on this day, he had a chair at the top of the stairs on the landing and said I couldn't rest until I reached that chair. I remember looking up and seeing how far away the chair was from where I was, then I remember looking at my legs thinking *nope, I need to quit right here. It's not going to happen.* I tried to turn around to slowly go back to my room, but Mum said she wasn't letting me past until I tried. I felt sorry for myself for a short while until I thought *okay, let's try.* My Mum stood behind me at the bottom of the stairs, walking closely behind as I moved towards the chair and Jos stood in front of me on the step above the one that I was standing on. I had the handrails for support if I needed it...which I did, so I walked up on the left-hand side as I couldn't use my right arm or hand yet, I needed to be on the side of my "good arm."

I was excited that I hadn't needed them to hold me up, but I could feel my body finding the smallest movement incredibly hard. It took a very long time and each movement that I made was tiresome. Words of encouragement came from Jos and my Mum, and these helped, it really helped because I wanted to give up so badly.

Step after step, I needed a few moments to catch my breath and take it all in. I think this may have taken around twenty minutes to walk these few steps, but I made it to the top eventually.

I MADE IT TO THE TOP!

YEAH, I WALKED. BRAIN, WE WILL DO THIS.

I was exhausted when I reached that chair, I sat down on it a for a short while, then looked at Jos and my Mum and stuttered or slurred through some dribbly words to basically ask how I was getting down. My brain was still recovering, so yes although I had just climbed what felt like a huge mountain, my brain didn't understand that I needed to be the one to walk back down the way I came up.

Shit.

That's a long way down. I will fall and hurt myself, I think I better stay put.

I was so scared when I sat on the chair at the top of the landing. I remember looking down and realising that for about a month, probably a bit longer that I had not walked down any stairs, not even a single step. In fact, my walking had been an absolute minimum because, well, I couldn't walk. This day was a huge day in the sense that it was the furthest I had ever walked since the stroke but also the first time I had walked up a staircase, even if it was only 6 steps. I mean, we all walk up and down the stairs every day, and it takes seconds, right? If you live in a flat and have no stairs just work with me here...there are stairs that at some point you would have walked down and it's just something your brain naturally tells your body to do. You don't even say to yourself "Hey brain you see all those steps, yeah we need to walk down them now." You literally just walk down them, without a single thought. Your brain is unaffected and wired correctly that it will do all the work for you, without you even realising what is even going on up in that beautiful brain of yours; it's pretty incredible.

Me walking those 6 steps up, then those same 6 steps back down took about an hour; it was such a tiring experience. Telling your brain to move limbs that still aren't registering as your own, holding on for dear life to the handrail and trying to breathe throughout this entire process - these are all normal parts of everyday life that most of us don't even need to think about. You know, breathing, walking, talking and generally just every single moment of your day that requires a movement.

After a stroke every element of normality is taken away. Everyone's recovery differs, some recover quicker than others, some might still be recovering and fighting for their lives every single second of the day and some may never have fully recovered. There is just no real answer to the question that I always thought of and often asked when I eventually learned new words and how to say them again.

"Will I fully recover?"

No one could answer that question, and no one could give me the answer that I wanted to hear, a simple three letter word.

Yes.

That word never got said. I survived the stroke, just about.

I was getting stronger and stronger whilst I was back on the Oncology ward. These small improvements to my speech and the even smaller steps that I made each day were getting better. I was getting stronger and slowly adapting to this new body that I needed to live in.
After the meetings that the doctors had amongst themselves with others from different medical backgrounds, came the time that my family needed to explain to me that I needed to move to a different place to get better. I just remember thinking '*oh, I don't get to go home yet?*'
I was faced with more fear, fear of again having to leave the Oncology. I mean the last time I left here I had a stroke. It seemed the Oncology was my safe place, safe from the outside world, my little bubble. If I left it, things just went from bad to worse. I am not sure how much worse they could have got if I'm honest as I had already been to hell but was still dragging myself back out of there.
After discussions amongst the family and me realising that I was no longer in need of chemo, so therefore shouldn't really take up bed space when someone else may need it, came the time to move on. Time to recover, *come on brain we can do this.*

Can we?

They said that I would need to go to Frenchay hospital, here in Bristol for more rehabilitation. *Okay* I thought to myself, I know where this is. That seems familiar, okay. I remember asking how long I would need to be in Frenchay for "for like a day or?" - turns out I needed to stay there until I was better and able to be more independent and look after myself. Again, at this point we still weren't aware of how much more I would be able to do or if my brain was too damaged to recover any further, but there is always hope. Before I had a place at Frenchay I needed to be assessed so that they knew the type of care I required and how they could help give me their utmost care. Assessment day was upon us, and I had no idea what was going on or why there was a stranger asking me so many questions or making me do things like stand up, because that took a lot of time, and these things were exhausting.

This stranger was called Doctor John Holloway, he was a Consultant Neuropsychiatrist at the Frenchay Rehab Centre and was the one who held my assessment. I remember he was taking notes on a little notepad, and I didn't understand what he could possibly be writing or where I was going.

Is this a test?

If I fail, will they not let me in? If I don't pass this test though does that mean my care ends and I will have to be pushed out of here in a wheelchair? I can't move a wheelchair alone though because I can't use my right arm or hand, so someone has to push me everywhere for the rest of my life? So much went through my head and it exhausted me just to think about the fact I was going somewhere new.

I really hope I pass this test.

The questions that were asked were simple things such as confirming my name, he jotted something down when I answered. I thought *oh no, have I failed because I dribbled, and it wasn't clear what I was trying to say. STUPID BRAIN WHY DO YOU HATE ME.*

Amongst answering a few questions, I also had to show him the limits of my movements, how many steps I could walk, how long I could stand unassisted. Which wasn't long at all. When he asked if I was able to move my right arm, my brain told my left arm to pick it up. Watching my right arm drop back onto the hospital bed after picking it up was such a surreal feeling, because that's just it. I didn't feel it. I spent a lot of time holding my right arm and carrying it with my left. The last and final thing he asked me, and I remember this question and moment vividly:

"Madeleena, I want you to draw a clock face. Then on that clock face I want you draw the time ten to two."

Huh?

What the heck is a clock?

EVERY little thing sent my brain into overdrive. When I looked at him, my brain then slowly reacted...I started looking around the hospital room. At first, I wasn't even sure what I was looking for, then I noticed Doctor Holloway jot some more notes on his pad, now I feel scared and pressured.

I must be looking around for this so-called clock. Then he jotted something else down and I saw he had a watch on his wrist. When he saw my face light up after noticing his watch, he wrote something else down.

AH HAH.

This clock thing must be round.

Round?

What am I drawing again?

I drew the worst circle I had ever drawn before and looked at him slightly proud of myself. He asked if I had finished, I looked down at the wonky red circle and thought *I must be missing something then*? I asked him to repeat what he asked of me. I asked a few times because I was tired from drawing the circle, exhausted and getting frustrated because my words weren't right.

"One."

Now is really not the time brain.

"Please draw a clock, with the time showing ten to two. Or 1:50 if that makes it easier?"

150? Huh?

I looked around again. Then I thought *ah! I need numbers on here, but where do they go?* I started feeling my emotions going wild and I wanted to cry. *What the hell is a clock? I mean it sounds like a simple task and I feel like I've been sat thinking about a clock a long time. TIME. That's what clocks do? Yes, I think this is the thing that tells the time!!*

WHAT IS A CLOCK?

Brain?

You there?

Hey...if you're listening can we try and work together because I don't know what is going on? This man seems important, and I think if we fail this test, well I think I might die again. If I die, we die. You are basically dead already, what do you say about drawing a clock, so we win this? I know you don't wanna die in there, I don't want to die again...I'm scared.

Please help me brain, hello?

Slowly my brain started working with me.

I drew the numbers 12, 3, 6 and 9...in that order.

Dr Holloway continued to jot notes whilst I wrote these numbers in. Then I struggled to work out where the other numbers needed to go, what those numbers might be and what order they needed to go in. I started stressing out and panicking, my parents were also in the room with us, and they said to take my time, that I could do it. I remember thinking, *do they know what a clock is?*

Can we cheat this test!?

It took about 10 minutes to hold this pen in my left hand, my brain was rejecting my body holding it as it knew it wasn't my dominant hand.

BRAIN, we need to use the left hand because I don't know where my right arm is, okay?

Slowly I scribbled in the 1, 2, 4, 5, 7, 8, 10 and 11...not in that order. Then I remembered 150. Whatever 150 meant, but I think I heard him say ten to two. I drew a line towards the two...and then my brain went into overdrive.

Here is what I drew on that very day during this assessment.

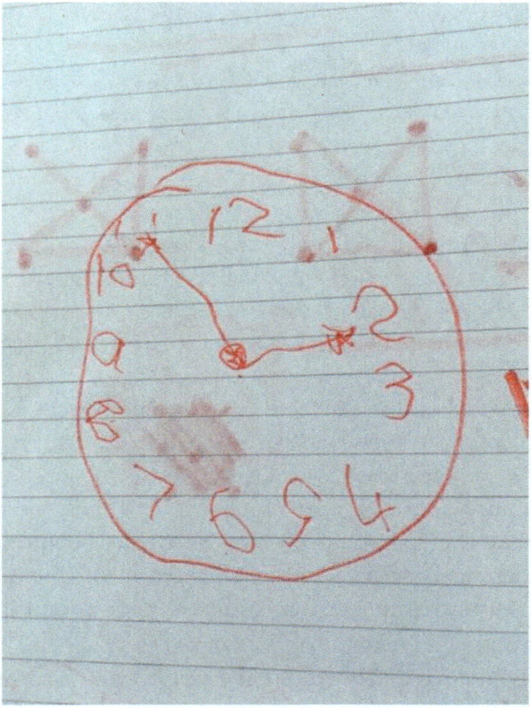

My writing here believe it or not was considered 'readable', sometimes it was just scribbling which in my brain appeared to be words.
My dominant hand as I said before wasn't recognised as my body yet, so from this point I had to adapt and become left-handed whilst my brain was recovering.
Dr Holloway thanked me for my time, said that I had done really well and then he and my parents went to discuss some other things further.

Hello? Did I pass?

Mum and Dad explained that in the next few days I will be moving to Frenchay to start my rehabilitation, but they would not be able to stay with me, I will have to stay alone.

Um. No, not okay with that. The last time I was left alone I had a stroke; I am not okay at being alone. Please tell me I failed the test.

Great. I passed it, nice one brain.

I was upset and scared that I would need to be left alone, really scared as at this point, I still had minimal speech and was still not able to eat a meal. There were so many questions going on in my head and I was really tired from drawing a stupid clock.
I wondered what this Frenchay place would bring me. Surely it has to offer me something other than fear, but not yet.
Over the next few days, I needed to have my groshong line removed before moving to Frenchay. This had been in my chest since the start before they started my chemotherapy. Now, this was only really designed to be in for the duration of my chemo treatment...four months. Well, 6 months later and my body had taken it on as its own.
This is where we discovered that I was able to scream. Holy crap did I scream.
I may have not been able to speak properly but Jesus could I yell, it was also the first time I was physically able to cry. What an absolute combination of chaos.
My Mum, Dad, Angel and everyone else in the room looked really upset to hear me scream in pain and to see me cry. I had been so quiet, so unlike me and now all I can do is scream. I thought to myself, *you know what leave it in as it clearly doesn't want to leave my body. I don't mind it, I'll keep it.*
I had several different doctors and nurses assisting, all of them attempting to remove it through my yelling, each one of them failing and realising they needed to give me more local anaesthetic.

GIVE ME MORE OF THAT DRUG! IT IS NOT WORKING. OUCHHHHHH. OUCHHHHHH.

I think Angel was basically passed out watching me and seeing all the blood, I had never seen her look so pale.
My Mum went to sit down with her and then Dad came and had his hand crushed to pieces by me instead. It was unbearable, I could not feel most of my body at this point but I sure as hell could feel this and it was not good.
It took a while to remove this small thing from my body, it's funny but I had become quite fond of it. That sounds really bizarre I know, but over the 10 months of being in and out of the Oncology and ICU it meant that I didn't need a nurse jabbing a needle into me every day. It also meant that after the stroke anything that was needed to be given to me quickly meant that there was already a vein accessible.
This brings me back to a time in the ICU when they ran out of space in my right arm for needles and so needed to go into my feet, EURGH. They had to keep my left arm clear of needles as it was the only limb that I was able to use to communicate. I have never squirmed so much; I didn't know that those feet were mine, but that needle was big, and I didn't want it going anywhere near those feet! They managed to wiggle it into my arm amongst the several other needles though, in the end. If I could have moved my foot, I probably would've happily kicked him in the face, as cute as he was. BACK OFF.
I needed to lie down in silence for a bit after they removed the Groshong line as it was all a bit traumatic. Most of my days were spent in silence as I couldn't really say or make anything make sense. I did smile though, once my not so pale sister and parents laughed and said, "well, you can scream again!" I left a slight smile with them, before passing out for a well-deserved sleep.

A few more days passed.

Then it was time for a new chapter in my life, Frenchay.

The Brain Injury Rehabilitation Unit.

CHAPTER 13

FRENCHAY

THE BRAIN INJURY REHABILITATION UNIT

11th December 2006, shortly after 2:30pm.

Frenchay, Frenchay, Frenchay.

Wish us luck here brain.

Everyone called this place BIRU for short. A lot of the information during my time at BIRU has been taken from my Mum's diary that she wrote whilst I was in Oncology, ICU and BIRU. We were just reminiscing and laughing at most of what she wrote. I am so grateful that she kept a diary as it has really helped me piece this chapter together which I would have struggled to do alone, thanks again Mum!

Now I don't remember the entirety of the day in which we travelled from the Oncology to BIRU but what I do remember is arriving, and I remember this well.

There was a barrier and you needed to speak to the intercom for the barrier to go up...of course this place was expecting me, so whoever spoke just had to say my name and up the barrier went. I had help to get out of the vehicle provided by Frenchay. By help I mean I was in a wheelchair, I was not able to walk myself out of the Oncology nor was I able to walk into this new scary place called BIRU. I still had the feeding tube in, so that needed to be wheeled alongside me too.

My parents and I walked in or got wheeled in respectively, we were met at the reception by several staff members and Doctor Holloway.

Please don't make me draw a clock again, I thought to myself. My parents had to sign into the visitor's book, which was a gentle yet forceful reminder that *'oh yeah...they aren't staying with me tonight'.* They each had to write their names, the date, and the time. Whilst they were writing in the visitors' book, I looked around, confused as to why it looked so festive and why there was tinsel everywhere. *What month is it?*

We were then shown past reception and I was wheeled down a corridor towards my room. It smelt different here, it smelt different to the Oncology...I don't think I'm going to like it here. It isn't that it smelt bad, it just didn't smell familiar, it smelt super clean, and not medical in the slightest. I never thought I would miss the medicinal smell of Oncology. Yet there I was, missing all the familiar faces and hospital smells. As I was taken to my room, I noticed other patients here too. This is one of the scariest things for me, something that haunts me even today. The patients in here were each suffering from several different types of brain trauma. For example, the guy in the room opposite mine had suffered brain injuries from a car crash, he dribbled too. He dribbled a lot, but I thought okay I dribble too, I understand you. What was nice is that he had people visiting him at the time, and they were laughing. I also thought what a nice sound it was that they were making, my brain didn't associate what this noise was until later, and that noise was laughter. What a beautiful sound. It made me wonder if I would ever be able to make that sound again.

My room was spacious; it had a single bed, a wardrobe, and a set of drawers. There was a long red emergency cord next to the bed. There was a bedside table and a light switch above the headboard. My door had a lock on it and a little window with a curtain on. There was a window in the room too which in the days, let in plenty of light. I tried my best not to look outside as I missed the outside world; despite being completely petrified of it at the same time.

I met a lot of staff that day and felt very overwhelmed and tired. I didn't want to leave this room, as everyone outside it really scared me. There was this young girl; she was maybe my age at the time perhaps even younger. She had this metal brace drilled into her head and it scared the life out of me, I was scared that if my brain didn't recover that I might need that too. Everything was crazy here in the first few weeks, it really took a long time to adjust, and I don't think I quite dealt with any of it until many years later.

With all these patients and new staff came new noises and new sounds. The staff were all lovely and they did their best to care for me and everyone else there, but I couldn't wait to leave.

After ten minutes of being in BIRU I was ready to go home.

The staff let me, and my parents familiarise ourselves with our surroundings. They said to my Mum that if I preferred, they could bring my own bedding from home and my own pillow, anything that they felt that might make my stay more comfortable.

You know what would've been more comfortable? Being at HOME in my OWN bed.

I wondered at the time if I would just need to be in there for a few days.

After my Mum and Dad packed away my clothes and things into the drawers, Mum started to explain where my toothbrush was and made sure it was somewhere my brain could remember, in plain sight.
I said bye to my Dad who went to wait in the car whilst my Mum got me changed into my pyjamas and helped me brush my teeth. I said bye to Mum and asked if she could stay, she said no and that I needed to be strong. She said they would both come and see me the next day.
It was getting late, by late it was maybe 9pm but I was extremely tired. Someone knocked on my door shortly after my parents left to ask if I was okay and if I would like a drink. She also asked if I would like to sit with the other patients in the living room. It was apparently movie night. I was thirsty so I nodded to that part, she came back in with the glass of water, and she asked me if I wanted her to put it in the living room with the other patients.

I said no.

I didn't want to see any of those people, they scared me, and I wanted to be alone. I stayed in my room and tried really hard not to choke on the water whilst keeping a close eye on the emergency cord in case I needed it. I was told I wasn't able to lock the door at night in case of an emergency, I was only allowed to lock it for example when I was changing; which I couldn't do alone yet anyway. Plus, my brain looked at this lock and didn't have a clue how to operate it. I was too scared to sleep, and there was so much going on in my head. There were so many new noises, and then there was nothing. With my brain in the state it was at the time, I cried. I cried to myself all the way through the night and into the next morning where I had the puffiest eyes ever.
The next morning, December 12th, 2006, around 10am a nurse knocked on my door and she asked if I would like her to help me get ready and dressed for the day, I politely

declined. She asked if I would like to go with her to make breakfast, but I didn't want to leave my room. She said if I didn't want to sit in the room with the others then she would sit in the kitchen with me away from the main room. I went with her to the kitchen, my left hand carrying my right arm, slowly dragging my feet the small steps towards the kitchen. I nodded when she asked if I would like toast, then I panicked because I wasn't sure if she knew that I would be unable to butter it. I panicked because everyone was new to me, *would anyone know that I am unable to do all these things, I can't talk properly and I'm too scared to tell them because they just won't understand me.* She asked if I would like to try and butter a slice of toast and helped place the knife in my left hand, to which I ended up buttering the plate. This really upset me, my brain wasn't telling my right hand to hold the toast in place, I just wanted my Mum. The nurse said it was okay and it would take time. She was so lovely, despite me not getting a single bit of butter anywhere near the toast. She buttered it for me, I ate my toast and swallowed each bite carefully (yeah you heard...I'm eating now! Even if it was cold toast that took 20 minutes to eat.)

She helped me walk back to my room where I saw my Mum and Dad; they had been here since about 10:30am. Mum helped get me washed and ready for the day as the nurse had mentioned I didn't want any help from them. I wasn't ready for anyone else to dress or wash me yet, no thank you. My Mum said I needed to try and let them help me as it is part of my recovery.

A nurse knocked on the door around 11am, she said to us all that she wanted to take the feeding tube out.

YOU WHAT.

The last thing I had taken out was the Groshong line and that hurt like hell, now this crazy lady wants to pull this thing out of my nose which is basically feeding me as I am unable to eat enough. *Is she crazy?* I remembered back to the time I ripped out my catheter after waking up from a stroke in ICU, despite not being able to feel anything down there. I was lucky to not have caused any damage internally. So, I'd better let the professionals take this out...

I looked at Mum and Dad worried and confused, another nurse came into the room to assist. If any of you have ever had one of these shoved down your nose it really isn't pleasant, right? I had to have about 3 of them overall. I had these in due to loss of appetite in the later stages of chemo, then because I was unable to chew or swallow after the stroke. Take a deep breath in Leena, they said. EURGH. A few deep breaths and a cough later they pulled this slimy tube out of my nose from deep within my stomach. GAG. For those of you that perhaps aren't grossed out and are intrigued it was called a 'Nasogastric Tube.'

Having that put into my nose was awful; having it taken out was something else. I did wonder if this was a good sign, as this provided all the nutrients I needed and stopped me from being dehydrated. *Does this mean that I am better? Will I be able to eat actual food soon? Something other than toast and soup? What even is food? Food comes from a bag, goes into my nose and down into my stomach, right?*

Well, that was slightly traumatic. The nurse said, "When you came in, I thought straight away that the feeding tube needed to go." I slurred a few words back which my parents loosely translated as "she's worried as she's unable to eat much, she wants to know if she will be okay without it?" The nurse looked at us all and smiled, it was reassuring.

She said she had reviewed my progress with the last Speech and Language Therapist from the ICU and Oncology and there had been great improvements. She said that I will learn to eat properly again, and I will eat enough to be able to have all the nutrients I needed without the feeding tube. She also mentioned that when I ate my toast earlier on it showed that I can eat and that I just needed to be careful.

A lovely lady came in after my feeding tube ordeal, around about 11:30am. Her name was Emma, and she was my Physiotherapist (PT). Mum left and said she would come back later in the afternoon to see how I got on with my first session. There were also talks of an early Christmas party that day at 2pm. Great. Explains the tinsel.

Emma said she wanted to assess me walking towards the gymnasium, which is where all the PT sessions took place. There were handrails alongside the corridors of BIRU so I stood near the left-hand side carrying my right arm. If you clench your right hand into a tight fist with the thumb tucked in, then with your left hand hold your right wrist. This is how I spent most of the time walking around, any time I needed to move I would carry my right arm. It felt heavy and it eased the load if I carried it around, my brain deemed this as normal. I would often walk into things, for example when I turned a corner too soon forgetting that I had the right side of a body…therefore walking into the wall. I walked into walls a lot or walked too closely to things on my right-hand side without realising. I spent a very long time carrying my right hand around like this, a very very long time. My right hand remained clenched as a fist for a few weeks. During my PT sessions Emma would have to use quite a lot of pressure and force to ease my right fingers apart, and to open my hand. I couldn't feel it when she did this, my brain and my body just fought against her. When I say force, she was careful in her sessions. It's hard to describe, but for example when she tried to move my index finger to help straighten it out, it just sprung back into the fist.

It took several weeks for me to tell my brain to relax my right hand, I didn't even realise that it would be possible to think of something and your brain eventually tell your body to do it.

That's just it, isn't it guys? We don't need to think about 'small' day-to-day tasks, right? If you dropped a pen, you wouldn't sit, look at it and tell yourself out loud to pick it up, your brain knows that its job is to send that message to your hand to pick it up. Simple right?

For anyone that has had a brain injury, simply picking up a pen can take anything from 5 minutes to an hour. That's right, I once spent an hour telling myself to pick a pen up with my right hand, but my brain kept sending the message to my left hand, ignoring the fact there was still a right arm attached to my body.

Emma mentioned that each week I would have a schedule. I cannot remember everyone's names, so I do apologise because you guys are the reason that I am able to do most of what I do now, you are the reason that I am able to type this and able to tell my story. There were so many lovely staff on hand, each one of you truly remarkable in your own right. Patient, caring, loving and the best at making my time in BIRU the best it could have been, given how low I was feeling.

BIRU team of 2006, thank you. I may have disliked you for making me do all the small simple tasks repeatedly, not realising you were helping me all those years ago, but I know now. Thank you. To the Filipino nurse who is the reason for the title of this book, Salamat po - thank you.

My PT session ended. In this session I walked a few steps and tried balancing on one leg at a time. This was hard; I didn't even manage two seconds.

Mum and Dad came back around 2pm for this party, they mingled and met the parents of the other patients and had nibbles. There was a lovely buffet, Mum came with me to hold my plate, as I was unable to hold my plate and put food on it at the same time. I pointed to a few things, and she popped them onto a plate. There was a lot going on and I wasn't sure if I would be able to handle so many people around me whilst I chewed so I sat in a corner of the room with my parents; away from everyone else. A few members of staff and parents spoke to us in the corner, but they could see I was struggling and felt very overwhelmed, so they

politely gave us space.
I had a huge issue after the stroke and more so at this moment in time with people being around me whilst I ate or looking at me whilst I was eating. As I was still getting to grips with eating, swallowing, and chewing with my face still drooping on one side, it was a messy ordeal. I felt like I was being judged and it sent me into a state of panic if I thought others were looking at me. It made me not want to eat in front of people or eat at all.
Later, that evening everyone had a roast dinner, everyone but me. I remember looking around at everyone picking up their knife and forks, using both hands and I cried. I cried because I was hungry, and I couldn't feed myself. My brain couldn't tell me to pick up my cutlery; I didn't understand why others could. There were of course staff on hand, the BIRU staff were attentive and so patient. The difference is I cried because I didn't want to be fed, but I also couldn't feed myself properly. I had a few mouthfuls of food with my fork in my left hand, but as I was so tired, I was struggling to keep the fork in my left hand. I kept on dropping the fork and well the right hand was in a clenched fist hanging to my side. I didn't enjoy struggling to try and eat, and I also didn't want anyone to help me eat, I just wanted to be able to feed myself. Was that too much to ask?
My Mum and Dad had left after the party for a few hours and had spoken to the staff about how upset I was when they came to visit me after dinner. They told my parents that I didn't eat anything and that I was struggling to eat when in the dining room with the other patients. They said as a one off that maybe they could treat me to a special lunch the next day.
My brother Ricki also came to visit, he told me about his day and asked how I was and looked around my room. It was nice to see him; he could tell I was upset about something, and my parents told him why I was a bit down that day. BFATT came about an hour later and everyone started

talking about KFC, which was making me hungry. We all played scrabble and then everyone left, my Mum got me ready for bed and said it would be a better day tomorrow.

December 13th, 2006.

The visiting hours here were 5-9pm. As I was a new patient and not settling in too well my parents were allowed to visit sporadically throughout the mornings, afternoons and then over time they just started visiting in the evenings.
The schedule that Emma mentioned earlier would consist of Occupational Therapy (OT), Physiotherapy (PT) and Speech and Language Therapy (SLT).
I had begun Physio and Speech Therapy sessions in Oncology and ICU, but not Occupational Therapy.
Claire was my OT, she helped me get dressed in the mornings, which threw me back to the days right after the stroke, feeling low because I had to have someone else dress me, a stranger. I didn't like that one bit.
I was 18 years old and so many doctors, nurses and all kinds of medical staff had seen me naked, had to wash me, clean up after me, see me at my worst and now they had to dress me, why the heck can my brain not handle this simple task? *I cannot live like this forever, but is that why I am here? To keep drawing clocks and learn to let people dress me.* I cried. I cried as she helped me pull my right arm through my sleeve, *whose arm is that anyway?*

I had no idea what an OT was or why she had to dress me in the morning. Oh yeah, that's right. I couldn't. Now an OT's role for those of you who may not know is to treat patients who may have suffered injuries or trauma to the brain, much like me and that brain of mine.
OT's help you improve, develop, and recover as much as you can, including re-learning tasks required for day-to-day life. She helped me try and retrain my brain to use cutlery. We

focused on trying to tell my brain to pick up a spoon. No luck on this day, I got upset sitting staring at a spoon and my right hand was not reacting in the slightest.
The first OT session was hard, as was the first of every other session I had to do; each one of them more draining and harder than the last.
After the morning sessions were over, it was now lunchtime. I didn't want to sit in the dining room with the other patients and so I asked if I was allowed to have my food in my room. IT WAS A GLORIOUS DAY my Mum and Dad knew how upset I was the night before and so they treated me to a KFC which we all shared and ate together in my room.
Now I understood why they were talking about KFC the night before. I didn't mind eating in front of Mum and Dad, as after all they had seen it all already, me dribbling whilst trying to keep the food in my mouth and not choke as I swallowed it.
They left shortly after lunchtime as I had a session in the afternoon. One of the nurses brought me ice cream as she thought I might enjoy it. I most certainly did, I often enjoyed the food that didn't require any chewing in the early stages. Callipo ice lollies were and will always be my favourite. Oh, and Twister ice lollies, but I still don't appreciate how much smaller they are these days.

<u>December 14th, 2006</u>

My parents visited at 1pm, BFATT came a couple hours later, and they all stayed until 9pm. In the daytime Dad helped me with my hand exercises that Emma had given me to work on in between sessions. I found it hard to motivate myself outside of my sessions with her and so my Dad would help me every time he came to visit. He also helped me stay positive, even when I didn't want to do them. Mum and Dad each took it in turn to help with these exercises. At times I would try and do them on my own, but I gave up after a few minutes.

I gave up a lot.

With my parents there and encouraging me I achieved more than I would have done alone. I honestly believe my recovery is at its best because of those around me, pulling me through even when I wanted to give up.
I remember thinking I know now that it is December, and if today was the 14th, that would make tomorrow my birthday. I did not want to spend my birthday in this place, nor did I want to be here at all. I found it hard at the time trying to help my brain understand that this place was somewhere where I would get better. My brain wasn't helping me much at all in understanding why I was there. I knew I wanted to go home, but I also knew I was in the best place to get better and to rehabilitate. It was a daily battle and struggle trying to link my brain and body together and to work with them, not against them.
Mum and Dad spoke to the staff about whether I might be allowed home for a few hours on my birthday. They said they would have to speak to Dr Holloway the next day before giving us a final answer.

December 15th, 2006 – My 19th Birthday!

My Mum, Dad and Vicky came to visit me around 11am. Mum had brought in presents that my friends had passed onto her, to give to me. Each one of them made me smile. I'll just add in here that the last time anyone outside of BFATT and my family had seen me was around early September. I had obviously been too unwell to see anyone after my last course of chemo, which then led onto pneumonia and then a stroke. I still wasn't in a good place, so I still didn't want to see anyone. I had people texting me and keeping in touch, but I was very unlikely to reply depending on how tired my left hand was from the day. It took a long time to write a text with my non-dominant hand and I didn't want to speak to anyone on the phone, as they wouldn't understand me. It was a lot for my brain and body to handle, I would struggle to hold the phone and write a text with one hand; especially as my brain was still understanding that I only had the left arm able to do anything at this point. My phone wasn't a touch screen either (if touch screens were around then?) and my left hand struggled to apply enough pressure to the buttons at this point. I would often drop the phone and spend up to 20 minutes trying to pick it up again. To those of you who may possibly have thought I was ignoring you then, I wasn't. I sure as hell cannot express the stress, pain, and emotion I went through each day, but I was ever so grateful for all your kind words at the time. My phone spent a lot of the time on the floor. It was nice to have birthday cards up in my room; it felt a little more like home. Mum, Dad, and Vicky had also brought me a mini fibre optic Christmas tree for my room. They had got me a profiterole cake too, but I was scared to blow the candles out in case I spat everywhere meaning no one else could have the cake. Mum picked a candle off and I blew that one out away from the cake, and yes, I spat all over her. Sorry Mum.

My parents and Vicky stayed in my room playing Scrabble and eating cake whilst I went to lunch. All the staff and patients sang happy birthday to me, and they got me a birthday card signed by everyone. Considering I tried my best to avoid everyone in here, it really was a pleasant surprise.

Dr Holloway came to tell us around 4pm that I was allowed to go home for a few hours. This was so exciting! As soon as I got home, I wanted to see my room. I missed it and I just wanted to see it and so I struggled up the staircase, we have steep steps at home and the handrail is on the right-hand side so I had nothing to hold onto. It was scary but I made it up them. Even if I did have to crawl part of the way. I looked at my room and wondered how long it would be until I would be able to stay in it again. After a few days Dad put a handrail on the left-hand side to make it easier going up and down the stairs, ready for when I would be allowed back home for good. I really missed being at home, Mum had decorated the house ready for Christmas, and I was sad that I wasn't able to decorate the tree with her like I usually would every year. This must have been why they got me my own tree, so I could decorate it. I remember thinking that I hadn't bought anyone Christmas presents but I was also unable to go out shopping. I did a huge online order with Boots making the most of their 3 for 2 on Christmas gifts. I remember panicking thinking that I wouldn't be able to wrap anything, nor did I know if I would even be home for Christmas to give the gifts to them myself. So, I opted for the gift wrap option where everything would be packaged nicely into gift boxes for me.

My family and BFATT were over for my birthday, and we had pizza delivered. It was so nice to be home and just not in a hospital, I missed evenings like this one. I went back to BIRU at 9pm, tired from the birthday activities. I was so grateful that Doctor Holloway allowed me to have a few hours at home on my birthday. Over the next few days, I had Luke, Vicky, Ricki, BFATT, Mum and Dad visiting on different days, there was never a day where no one visited me. It helped keep me going, it kept me alive. Mum was still having to help me get dressed for bed but as time went on, I became more and more able to lift my arm a little higher or pull the top over my own head. Don't get me wrong, this took weeks to do but I did get there.

On the evening of 21st December my family treated me to Burger King. I had onion rings, a cheeseburger, and fries. It was delicious! I was really enjoying these treats and became more and more able to eat, chew and swallow like a normal person. It wasn't all takeaways and junk food by the way...but they were a great treat in between all the healthy meals.

I became more confident and started eating with the other

patients. Day by day starting with just breakfast, then lunch and then gradually I was eating all my meals with them. I don't think they ever really communicated with me; it might be that they were unable to, or it may be that they felt exactly the same as me. Scared and confused. Just praying that we each got better. There was a patient called Annabelle, and she was so sweet. The only way she was able to communicate with me at the time was with a smile, or laughter. If you ever read this, I hope you are as well as you can be and still smiling. Thanks for being kind to me, even if we never exchanged more than a few sounds.

Doctor Holloway discussed with my family that it could be an option that I am allowed home at the weekends. He said it really lifted my mood being home for a few hours on my birthday and he thought it may bring that positivity to my sessions if I go home over the weekends. There were no sessions on the weekends at BIRU, so it kind of made sense. I also remember getting excited because it was Christmas soon.

Does this mean I am allowed home for Christmas?

I went home on Saturday 23rd December 2006. The Boots Christmas presents I had ordered had been delivered and there were A LOT of parcels. My family moved them underneath the tree, all of them gobsmacked that I had thought about them during such a hard time.

Guys, if you know me – you'll know that I love buying gifts for others or making other people smile if I can. I had forgotten that I did this until reading my Mum's diary with her the other day. I felt so happy that I was able to get everyone presents, it is my favourite time of year because everyone is together - gifts or not. Christmas to me is just magical, and I think it always will be. Being able to spend it at home with my family whilst recovering meant a lot.

Sunday 24th December 2006

Angel had come over from Sheffield to see how I was getting on and to spend Christmas with us all. We had pancakes for breakfast, I had really wanted them since the moment I was able to eat again. We all played scrabble, Vicky and Luke came over too. It was the best weekend; my first weekend home since before the stroke.

Being at home on Christmas day was just amazing. I have always appreciated it ever since this day, because not being at home surrounded by your loved ones is awful, but there I was…home for Christmas. I remember thinking how lucky I was because home wasn't far from BIRU. However, many of the patients in BIRU at the same time as me were so far from home or too unwell to leave over Christmas. I was lucky, in more than one sense of the word.
On the evening of December 26th my Mum called BIRU to see if I would be able to stay home for another night, I had done hand exercises with Dad in the day. BIRU said it would be fine if I was back at lunchtime the next day for my sessions.

December 27th, 2006

I had some early afternoon sessions and Doctor Holloway spoke to me about potentially being allowed home over New Year's Eve. I felt very lucky and of course couldn't wait to tell Mum and Dad…but they already knew and had been keeping it from me.

December 29th, 2006

Each session differed day to day:

OT sessions these were repetitive, they had to be in order

to engage my brain and to train my body into sending signals to my right hand not just the left. All the sessions needed to be repetitive in order to engage my brain. These sessions helped improved my sensory and motor abilities, so I was able to one day get back to normality. These involved tasks such as using a computer, cooking and day to day care of myself, which meant having someone brush my teeth, wash me, and dress me until I was able to do this myself.
Using a computer in the beginning was difficult as my mind was unable to handle multiple things going on, I struggled with concentration, and it took a long time to get used to using a computer again. I typed with one finger for a few weeks and then became able to type with more than just the index finger. My right hand was unable to help, but if I placed my middle finger of my right hand on the enter button, it was able to apply pressure ever so slightly.
PT sessions these involved walking further each day, trying to cycle on a static bike, which believe me is very difficult when you aren't balanced correctly; I struggled to stay on it at times. There were balancing exercises to do, working on my balance was bizarre and tough. My brain was so disconnected when I first arrived in BIRU that it often would just give up on my legs supporting me, turning them into a jelly-like state. Each step I made was a step to me becoming stronger. There was a lot of physical activity involved within PT sessions to help preserve my muscle strength and to improve my energy levels.
SLT repeating certain words or sounds became easier over time, and I became able to string together proper sentences and start making small conversations with people. Once I got over the fear of how slurry my words were, I became comfortable in the fact that this may just be how I needed to sound to everyone from then on, so I had to get used to it.

This is quite possibly one of the greatest things that my Mum had written in her diary. "Leena held a spoon for the first time today in her right hand."

YES!!!!

I remember this day very well and I remember the reaction from Claire when I held a spoon in our session. Claire was ecstatic, I had spent almost the entire month of December telling my brain to reach for that goddam spoon; I did it guys.

I held a frickin' spoon!

December 30th 2006

Wahoo! I was allowed home for New Years; I was really excited that I would be allowed home again for the weekend. Often when I was allowed home, I would go with BFATT to see his parents. On NYE I went to see them for a few hours. They were so lovely, and they didn't judge how I looked, how I ate or how I spoke. They helped me in ways very similar to how my parents looked after me, and this made all the difference. BFATT's Mum would often cut my food up for me as I was unable to, this happened over the next few years. I was too scared to leave BIRU or my house, or to see anyone. However, they made seeing them so easy, and I had forgotten why I was so scared in the first place. As my confidence grew BFATT tried to find ways to encourage me to leave the house. I would often go with my parents and BFATT to supermarkets, but I would stand very close to them; using them as a shield to hide behind. I remember once BFATT said he wanted us to go to the cinema, and I was petrified at the idea of this. He reassured me that it would be a good thing to do. He said it not only gets me out in public to build my confidence that little bit more, but if I'm really worried at least once I was in the screening it would be dark, and everyone would be focussing on the film. We went to the cinema a handful of times, and it really did help build up

my confidence.
It was nice to be home for a few nights again. On January 1st, 2007, I had PT with Emma in the morning, and I felt the sessions were starting to pay off. I felt a lot stronger in myself and my coordination seemed to be better too. On the 2nd of January 2007 I managed to have a shower with less help from Claire, that's right I no longer was crying or only allowing my Mum to help me wash. In the beginning my Mum and Claire would both help me shower, but as time went on Claire took over and I just had to accept the fact I needed help.
Accepting that I needed help, or need help is a big deal. It was a huge deal in the early stages but now if I have to accept that I cannot do something I will ask for help, even if I don't want to. Claire gradually needed to help me less and less, but I still needed her to squeeze the shower gel into my hand occasionally, or to wash my hair.

Monday 8th January 2007

At 12pm Mum and Dad took me back to the Oncology for a Bone Marrow Harvest test (or a Bone Marrow Biopsy). This was a routine check-up that I needed to have done up until the 5 year all clear mark. I had so many of these tests, you'd think I would have got used to them, but I didn't. As much as I disliked them, I was often glad to have them done because it meant with usual check-ups, we were all aware of what may be going on in my body. What I learnt over having so many of them was that Mum needed to wait in the waiting room, whilst Dad would hold my hand throughout the test. Mum could often hear my screaming from where she was sitting, but at least she wasn't pale and almost passing out on us. My Mum spent so long seeing me suffer and go through so much pain, as did my family and BFATT and as did many of you. I have no idea how she managed sitting with me through so much, but the Bone Marrow Biopsies were always too much for my Mum to see, it was as my Dad said, "a really big needle". Remember when I left Oncology at the start of December? When I had to leave in a wheelchair, because I was unable to walk? Well. I walked in on this day.

Yes, without help.

I WALKED IN.

There were a lot of familiar faces, and everyone was so happy to see how much I had progressed. It was really nice seeing everyone and I felt so happy and comfortable, even though it was overwhelming. Dr Evely even came to see how I was doing; it was a really nice day. It was also nice to have a few hours away from BIRU. After the Bone Marrow Biopsy was done, I headed back to BIRU shortly after 3pm.

Tuesday 9th January 2007

This was a scary day. Today's OT session was one step further than picking up a spoon (which was pretty tough!) Today I had to get on a bus, public transport. PUBLIC? That means people, other people, strangers. That means more people will stare at me. Now this task wasn't set out to scare me, but it did. It is a simple thing that most people do and do without thinking. Not for me. I couldn't even think straight because my brain robbed me of that in this current moment in time. I was just in a state of panic.
The plan was to get a bus to Downend (an area here in Bristol), to then go to a shop called Somerfield (currently now a co-op). Then once we were in Somerfield, I had to buy a meal that I could prepare myself to have for dinner that evening.

Sounds simple right?

WRONG.

My brain went into overdrive when Claire explained what we would be doing that day. I had so much going on in my head. I couldn't remember how you stopped a bus, which direction I needed the bus to go, how I would hold a purse and count money out at the same time, *how much is a bus journey? What if the driver doesn't understand me? What do I even say to a driver about where to go? How do I stop the bus? FOOD?* After all this I also have to go into the busy supermarket, have people stare at me whilst I try and work out what I want to eat?!
This might all seem ridiculous and simple to you guys, but for a stroke survivor it isn't simple. Nothing after a stroke is 'simple', not for a very long time and for other people recovering, maybe never.
I told Claire that I was scared, and she reassured me that she would be there every step of the way. She would be in her work uniform, so at least hopefully this would make people realise that I am a patient and to understand why I am a mess. She said I didn't need to cook a meal from scratch, the aim of this task was to help me adjust to getting back to normality. She wanted me to get a microwaveable meal, the aim here was to follow instructions. To see if my brain could understand instructions and put them into action.

Here goes nothing.

Claire told me that we needed to get the number 5 bus and she took me to the correct bus stop, so I didn't need to worry about that part. There was an elderly couple at the stop already and Claire asked them if they wouldn't mind me stopping the bus instead of them. This was scary, but the bus stopped with whatever hand gesture I was attempting. Claire let the couple on before us, it is a good thing too because I took ages with this next part. Claire had some coins in a money bag, she passed me the money bag and said to me what I needed to ask the driver. All I needed to say was "one return to Downend please", but I was scared. I tried to, but

it came out "Downend." He couldn't make out what I said, and so I said it again but even quieter. I looked around and the people on the bus were annoyed at me and agitated, I started crying. I heard someone on the bus tell the strangers around her that I was a patient and to just give me time. Thank you, stranger, for your kind words and patience that day. That was such a kind thing to do, and the driver was aware due to Claire's uniform. I suppose with the bus stop being right outside BIRU they were probably used to it, but I wasn't. This was all new and scary. Claire told me to speak again but slowly, so I did, and the driver understood me. He told me the amount and I struggled with the money. Claire held the money bag for me whilst I dug around it with my left hand trying to recognise the coins.
After what felt like an hour, I finally got my ticket. Claire asked the driver if he could kindly wait until I was seated before he drove off as I was still unbalanced. Claire told me when to press the button to stop the bus. When I saw the shop, I was scared at the size of it. I thought there were going to be so many people inside. I walked in, carrying my right arm and walked aimlessly around the fridge aisles, I had forgotten what I was looking for. Claire said I needed to stop carrying my arm as how am I going to hold the food? Good question, *I have no idea? Should I know?*
I finally found the microwaveable ready meals, I looked at her confused and then looked back at the shelves, there was so much. I didn't know what to do. She told me that she wanted me to get a drink to go with it too. I picked up a tuna pasta bake that looked okay, then I dropped it. I looked at Claire, she said maybe I should get something to carry everything in as I might struggle to carry the drink too. *Ah, yes, what are those things?*

Baskets, that's it!

I picked up my pasta bake from the floor and wandered

around looking for a basket. Once I saw them it took my brain a little longer to work out why I was staring at a basket. I put the ready meal in, then picked it up. Now I had to find a drink, back to the fridges I go. I couldn't work out how to get a drink off the shelf and into my basket because my brain only thought I had one arm at this point. I eventually, with prompts from Claire, placed the basket on the floor, then placed my drink inside it with the ready meal.

Now. The tills.

Deep breath.

I placed my items on the belt, this took ages; working with one arm and hand was and is difficult. When I eventually placed the items down, I then panicked realising I needed to pack them away. The kind man asked if I needed help packing, Claire looked at me and said that I should try. Packing items into a bag proved difficult, I struggled to open the bag. Then I realised whilst I was struggling to open the bag and pack things into it one handed, I also needed to pay! There was so much going on, this was so hard and so tiring. People behind me in the queue were getting impatient, Claire told me to ignore them and to focus on what I was doing. She held the bag open whilst I put the items in, then I struggled to pay as my left hand was so tired that I dropped the coins everywhere. The guys behind me started moving their shopping to a different till.

To the people behind me in that shop on that very day I really hope you have learnt to have more patience in your life because this small action caused me a lot of pain. Of course, if you are in a rush and need to get about your days I understand, but to those of you out there reading this just give things maybe a second thought, you know nothing about the people around you day to day. You know nothing of their struggles and what they may be going through, so if you can, be more patient and be kind, always.

We had to get the bus back to BIRU, I sat in silence most of the journey and Claire said how well I did. She said not to worry about the people that were behind me, and that people are just in a rush when you should embrace and take each moment as it comes. She was so kind and so amazing that I smiled, because she was with me, I knew I wasn't crazy. I was just different, and she didn't care about how long I took. Once we got back to BIRU, she needed to assess me with the meal that I had bought. *A ready meal that goes into the microwave, right?* Nope, wrong again. *What the heck is a microwave?* My brain was shouting at me. I stared at the instructions on the pack, looked at Claire and then stared at the microwave. I repeated this for about 5 minutes. My mind was confused. Claire suggested that reading it out loud might help. I read it out about 8 times and then eventually worked out what I had to do to cook it inside this device they called a microwave. What should have taken 7 minutes took about 27 minutes as I had to really think about what the hell was going on. I felt really proud of myself after as I managed to cook something and follow instructions, I did it!

The following day I heard a knock on my door, it was a sweet lady with a HUGE dog! I was so excited; it was a St Bernard. They often take animals, mainly dogs, into BIRU as part of rehabilitation. He was a therapy dog and he made me smile; I didn't care that he was drooling all over my floor. I asked if I could stroke him and said he looked like Beethoven. Claire was with the lady, and she said I could stroke him, but it had to be with my right hand. MY RIGHT HAND STROKED THE DOG, I thought long and hard about this, but my right hand moved towards the dog. Now I couldn't tell how much pressure I was applying to the poor dog's head and at some point, I'm sure I slapped him by mistake, but he sat down and moved his head closer to my hand and licked it. I couldn't feel the lick, but it was so encouraging that he wanted me to stroke him again, so I did. WITH MY RIGHT

HAND. The lady took Beethoven (I forgot his name) to go and see the other patients and Claire took us to the therapy room for our session. I loved photography (still do) and so in this session it was to practice pressing the shutter button with my right index finger. It took about half an hour, but I took my first photo with my right hand. This was a great day.
As I was now getting stronger, Claire and Emma had mentioned that they wanted me to try Hydrotherapy. The next day Mum brought in my swimming costume, and on January 13th, 2007, I had my first Hydro session! I loved it, I felt invincible which sounds absolutely insane, but it really was the nicest feeling. It was the most incredible my body had felt since the stroke. It was the first time I felt my entire body as one again.
Hydrotherapy for those of you who may not know is a heated swimming pool in which physical therapy can take place.
Emma got me to do hand exercises in the water, and my brain reacted to this session incredibly. The exercises seemed effortless whilst I was in the water. I was held up with help from Emma and Claire and there were floats around me which we used within exercises too.
If you know anyone that has suffered a stroke or perhaps would benefit from improved mobility – water is your friend! It was scary looking at the water as my constant fear was that I might drown as I am unable to swim without the use of all my limbs, but once I was in the water I felt like a completely new person, I felt like a new me. Even though I had people keeping me afloat, it was the most independent that I had felt in a long while.
From this session onwards I started referring to myself as Nemo, this made everyone laugh, and I still refer to my right hand as my lucky fin.
On the 16th of January 2007 there was a review with all the medical team at BIRU, Doctor Holloway and my family. I joined the meeting a bit later. The meeting took place at 1pm, it was to discuss my progress with the PT, OT and SLT.

When I joined the meeting, they told me that the meeting was to discuss when I might be able to be discharged. They said my progress had really improved and that I was doing really well, however they still felt I would benefit with these sessions a bit longer but understood that I wanted to go home badly. They said if I continue to push myself to the best of my abilities then they would be able to review my progress at a later date. It was exciting to hear about the possibilities of going home, I was quite deflated at the end as I thought I might be going home that day.

Later that day I had my FIRST visit from some of my friends, now as I had mentioned earlier no one apart from BFATT and my family had seen me since early September, so I was petrified. *What if they didn't recognise me or want to be my friend anymore?* The friends that visited this day were Sophie, Laura, and Sandee. Sophie & Sandee are still two of my closest friends today, so I guess it didn't go too badly at all did it?

I have known Sophie for years, probably since we were 4. Our brothers are also best friends with each other. Any communication to my friends was usually from Ricki through to Sophie's brother Zak or from BFATT.

Having them visit me shouldn't have been as scary as my mind was making it out to be, but it was so scary I wanted to cancel; I am so glad that I didn't. I walked over to the reception area when Sandee or Sophie texted me to say they had arrived. I saw them signing into the visitors' book, and then Soph looked up, straight at me...and I just started laughing. We both started cracking up, then I forgot why I was scared. There was a reason we were laughing, but that's just for us to know – what you need to know is that she was laughing with me, not at me.

If you know me, once I start laughing, I often find it hard to stop. You know the proper deep laughs where you basically can't breathe anymore and make all sorts of ugly faces and noises? Yeah...you know. Once the staff realised, I was okay and not actually unable to breathe I showed my friends to my room, carrying my right arm along the way. They all had a look around my room and sat on my bed and we spoke. They were very patient with me and let me take my time to speak or asked me to repeat things if they didn't understand the first time. I was okay with repeating myself because they didn't laugh at me, it just felt...normal. I hadn't felt normal for such a long time, it was just such a relief - I love you guys. They left after an hour or so, I got myself dressed for bed one handed and brushed my own teeth.

The results of the Bone Marrow Harvest came back the next day. They told my parents that the results were good and showed no cancerous cells, yesss!!

I went home for the weekend and on January 21st Sandee and Rosie came to visit me at home, they brought over Doritos, dip and I think we may have watched Finding Nemo. I was able to open the door to them and I was slowly beginning to stop carrying my arm around.

On January 26th there were discussions of me potentially leaving BIRU, the staff were in and out of a few meetings. There were talks about further rehabilitation and treatment if I was to go home anytime soon. Treatment would not just stop as there was so much more recovery that I could potentially achieve but may not achieve this alone. They said I would benefit with more help from a rehabilitation team to achieve and hopefully gain more strength and mobility.

January 29th, 2007, my Mum's diary reads:

"Leena held a glass in her right hand and lifted it for a few moments."

This was even more exciting than holding a spoon. I not only lifted that glass with no contents in, but I also even lifted it with water in it and was able to hold it long enough over time to take a few sips out of it. This all took some time and really tested my brain. This simple task of holding a glass in my

right hand took hours of practice with plastic cups. Luckily, they were smart enough to use plastic cups because I would've smashed hundreds of glasses overtime. I did it, after a long time of persevering, I held that glass with my right hand, and didn't smash it.
On the 1st of February 2007, BIRU held a leaving party, this leaving party was for one of the patients. She was called Madeleena Takooree.

That's right, this leaving party was for me, ME!

I was finally discharged on Friday 2nd February 2007, after 52 intense long days like you could never imagine. Hours of retraining my brain and body to work as one. Sleepless nights, tears of joy, tears of sadness, feeling alone, feeling overwhelmed, feeling positive. Mixed in with feeling happy, sad, angry, frustrated, and broken, it was finally my time to go home.

CHAPTER 14

I'M HOME

I'm home.

Wow. There's nothing quite like being at home is there? I mean, when you have been in and out of hospitals for 10 months and have no real idea of what home even is after a stroke, it was a relief to be home. However, once I was home it didn't mean that I had fully recovered from the stroke. I had a long way to go.

My speech had improved a great deal and I was becoming more and more confident and independent. Sometimes I often got lazy and slurred my words as I knew my parents would piece together what I was trying to say. My family and BFATT knew that they needed to help me improve my speech further, so they often wouldn't respond unless I spoke properly. Now this might sound harsh, but I assure you it wasn't in the slightest. This action never upset me; it frustrated me but that's because my brain was really struggling. Without my family doing this you wouldn't understand a single word I say today. Thank you all for helping me get my voice back. As I needed to carry on the rehabilitation, I had an intermediate care team come to my house and assess me with day-to-day tasks once I had been discharged from BIRU. They watched me make a cup of tea during one session and because the sensation comes and goes in my right hand (at this point there was no sensation) I had to be really careful. You could have poured boiling hot water onto my right arm; my brain was so disconnected from it that I wouldn't feel it, but it sure as hell would burn and react the same as anyone else's body would.

Making a cup of tea with people watching you is daunting, having every movement analysed for such a long time proved very testing. It is something I found hard getting used to, but overtime just had to deal with it.

There were three people assessing me from the care team. They came over the next few weeks, I do not remember all their names; I do however remember the Physio's name. She was called Daisy and she was such a positive soul, she made me want to keep going and stay positive.

What was interesting was that I believe the three of them were in their early stages of this being their career, and still studying and so they had never come across anyone with limited movements such as mine face to face yet. I did think, *should this scare me?* They were so fascinated and so invested that they really wanted to help. They showed me a ton of exercises that I could do around the house with my parents' help and ones that I could do on my own. One of the tasks that they got me to do at home was to practice speaking on the phone, something I often tried to avoid. They wanted me to call a local company and just ask their opening hours.

Again, I know this is a simple task, but it really was difficult. Difficult not only to physically dial the buttons but then to remember what I needed to ask. I tried a few times, the first time I hung up when the gentlemen answered (sorry). Then I tried a few more times and succeeded. They were all so proud of me and I was proud of myself. These small steps made up who I am today, without any of these 'simple' daily tasks I wouldn't have very much of myself left at all. They came several times; they were allocated time to help me rehabilitate until I was able to be looked after by the Head Injury Therapy Unit (HITU). Now HITU was at Frenchay, on the same site as BIRU. The difference here was I just needed to go in for my sessions during the appointment time I was given and then I got to go home again after, ah home. Home, sweet Home.

At HITU I still had PT and OT sessions (I still may have had speech therapy, but I can't remember). The main things with OT were trying to hold a pen and to tell my brain that its dominant hand is the right and not the left. There were also tasks where I needed to type out sections of a book onto a pc with my right hand. It took about twenty minutes to write a sentence, at this point I was only able to type with one finger, my middle finger. Everyone used to laugh when we first started noticing that this was the strongest finger, I must've sworn a lot before the stroke maybe, haha.

My PT sessions by now meant that I had more of a range of movement, and I was also no longer carrying my arm around. It took months to train my brain and to tell it that it did not NEED to carry my right arm and it took several months to stop walking into things on my right side. My Mum, Dad, BFATT or anyone in the family that was around but mainly my parents drove me everywhere.

To numerous appointments often at different times or days each week, but it never phased any of them. They wanted me to get the best recovery possible and I know that they would have done anything for me if I needed it, and they did. They still do, my family and friends are incredible much like I think you guys reading this would think the same of your loved ones. Often, we can forget how much others do for us, and during 2006 – 2011 and even now my family did everything in their power to make sure I am here today. I was pieced back together with the incredible help of the NHS but my family who saw me every day and not once gave up on me. I would not be here today without you and I sure as hell wouldn't be able to write this. My friends and BFATT played a huge part in my recovery too as without them I would have felt even more alone than I already did. To feel like I was the only person to suffer like this was difficult, of course there are undoubtedly people in the world that are far more worse off than me and I will never doubt that for a minute; but this is my story, and I had a tough time.

To say 'tough' is an absolute understatement but there aren't enough words. If you saw me go through it, then you'll know; no words would be required. If you are reading this and perhaps are comparing my story to your own, no two stories are the same, no two cancer patients will have the same story and no two brain injuries are the same. No one can tell you what will happen after a stroke or how long it will take until you are able to go home, or if you'll ever go home again. What I do know is that my parents and family were told to prepare for the worst one day, then told I would never walk again. So, prove them wrong and try your best to be the best version of yourself if you ever hear that. I not only walk but I run when I can, because why wouldn't I? I mean the 5:30am runs me and Vicky used to do every morning when I was healthier and more fit were probably not necessary, but they also were. It always feels so great to run after being told in 2006 that I may never walk again. There is always hope and I class myself as lucky, I really am lucky to be here and to have so many amazing people in my life.

I enjoyed going to sessions at HITU and being an outpatient. I mostly loved that I was able to go home after. The sessions were hard, but I wanted to progress and please not only myself but those putting in the work to help me. I also went to the Bristol General Hospital for sessions although the time scale of this is a bit uncertain. What I do know is that Jos worked there, remember him from Oncology? The reason I was able to walk again, that's the guy. Me, my Mum, and Dad all smiled when we saw Jos walk through reception and he

was amazed that I had managed to walk in by myself. He was also amazed by my speech and said how great it was that I was having a conversation with him. That's right guys, without the dribble too now!
My time at HITU was hard, the exercises differed to those in BIRU as I had gained more strength in my right arm and hand and so they needed to challenge me more day by day. I remember one day the PT opened a deck of cards and I remember thinking *what are we playing?* They wanted to find ways of me lifting my arm up to help regain movement and strength in different ways. The task I had to do was to hold a single card flat against a wall, as high as I possibly could with the fingertips on my right hand.

SIMPLE…NOPE!

I needed help from the PT to help spread my fingers apart as my brain reacted in a way that it freaked out, it clenched into a fist. My body often went against these little tasks, for example when I tried to open my hand from a fist, it just got into a tighter fist, when I tried to relax my hand, it just became more tense. Rewiring your brain is difficult, never-ending, and tiring, it is also fascinating at the same time.
Most of us don't think about what we are doing when we do them, however for myself and many other stroke survivors it's a constant thought. Each thing we do in the early stages is to try and piece everything together, our brains are over flooded but at the same time completely empty in seconds.
For me personally, after having to think about something for so long before I was able to do it became the norm, it then became difficult to adapt and have my brain react on its own. It's a bizarre thing to try and explain so I apologise if it makes no sense. For example, you are reading this aren't you? I would have had to read words over and over again for up to an hour at a time before my brain registered any of them. It isn't a quick recovery after a stroke and each exercise I had

to do repeatedly became easier over time, but time. Time is what we need to heal and recover. It took an incredibly long time to work out how to tell my brain to relax but more importantly how to do this without getting frustrated and crying.

The next session at HITU they had a huge jack of spades card, A4 size which they wanted me to try instead of a standard size playing card. To start off with something that my brain hopefully would deem as easy and then to make it harder as I progressed.

Whilst this huge playing card should've been easier to hold, it was the same story. My fist held the card in place, not my fingertips or the palm of my hand. As the sessions went on and my hand started to relax, I became able to do it and I then overtime managed to do this with a standard size playing card. I only managed to hold it with my right palm but not for very long before it clenched back into a fist.

One other session with the OT I remember was a reaction test, they wanted to see how quickly my brain reacted and how long that message took to reach my body. On the PC they set up this test where I had to tap the spacebar on the keyboard every time the letter 'Z' appeared on the screen. They first tested my left hand's reaction time and then they tested the right hand. Obviously, the right hand was slower but also what was interesting is that I don't think my left hand was much quicker. My brain struggled for a long time to send messages to what I call my "good arm" (the left) and so daily tasks were always a long process and frustrating. Constant frustration because not being able to do something that you used to do was hard and the thought of never drumming again hit my mind.

If you remember at the start of this book, I mentioned I was in a band called Incured. Yeah, random band name and it isn't even a word...we know. At a band rehearsal they had misspelt 'Incurred' and we thought it would make a cool band name. I don't care what anyone says, we were cool. I

remember one day just thinking *crap, there are days I can't even brush my teeth by myself or cut my own food, will I be able to drum again?'*
At the time the other guys in the band - Mark, Steve & Rosie were still writing or doing their own thing until I got better. We also had to be realistic though, I had been out of action for ten months and unable to look after myself, unable to walk, talk or do things that I used to do. We used to have band rehearsals every Sunday for four hours, song writing sessions midweek, every week. Then gigs, man I loved playing gigs! We usually played somewhere weekly, but the gigs picked up to the point where we were like "man, we are going to have to write new material faster!" Even though we were this small four-piece unknown (outside of our many friends and local bands at the time) emo band, it was amazing when people in the audience knew every lyric, I think they knew the songs better than me.
During chemo we spoke a bit as a band about what would happen and it was always going to go back to "normal" after treatment had ended, and I was well enough to play again. Gigs would resume and life would carry on as before. Then came pneumonia and a stroke making normality non-existent. We all spoke about how I was recovering a few months after the stroke but naturally they all ended up doing their own thing during my chemo or going their separate ways into solo gigs or other bands.
At HITU each day differed as to how much I was able to do in the sessions. If I was tired, the exercises were a lot harder to achieve as my brain was slower to react. I found it hard sleeping after the stroke and then on and off for a few years. In the early days I tried not to sleep as I was scared, scared that I would wake up in the ICU again. For a long time, the fear of having another stroke really affected me. Of course, we can't say what is going to happen in the future and I soon learnt that I couldn't live like that, sleeping is everything your mind needs to heal and recover, not just for a stroke survivor

but for all of us. Having said that, it took a long time to let myself rest but with the sessions and the hard work I put in, it drained me so much that I slept very well during this time. As my right side of my body felt numb constantly, I had been advised by the staff that at night I should try and avoid sleeping on my right arm. Due to the bad circulation in my arm at the time they advised me to try and avoid lying on the right side the best I could. The circulation was so bad that during winter my fingertips would go blue whilst the left hand was warm and not affected. I often wore one glove to try and balance this out, looking like a weirdo. At night I slept with my arm in a splint to help regain its neutral position, it was very confusing to my mind and often I would take it off in my sleep without realising. Forcing a limb to go into a neutral position when it has forgotten how to act was very painful and sore at times, and uncomfortable at night for quite some time.

I slept on my right side for years up until the stroke, so trying to force myself not to lie on my right side was hard. You know when you've slept funny on your arm and your body goes a bit numb and limp? Think of that x 100 every day. That is what it felt like after the stroke and how my right arm felt. At times I didn't feel it or know it was even my arm (during my time in ICU & BIRU), then I kept falling asleep on it, thinking each morning that I had suffered from another stroke. Each morning when I woke up for around two years I would speak, or just say a word just to make sure I still had a voice. In fact, I often still do that even to this day.

I went to HITU for several months until I hit the most recovery I could have achieved. The sessions at HITU were limited but they did continue for a few months before ending. I still had the exercises to do at home and I also had numerous Physio sessions in Hengrove here in Bristol a few years later.

My sessions at HITU were hard and I was often given exercises to take home and do in between sessions, I really struggled with these. My Mum, Dad and BFATT would help me with them. I struggled to focus and do these on my own, often I would say I had done them for the day when I hadn't. They could tell I was lying, but it was hard guys. I won't lie to you now, it was hard. I lied a handful of times about doing the exercises and of course it was obvious I hadn't because I don't like lying and whilst I thought this little lie would do no harm, it also did no good. Lying about doing these 'simple' exercises made me no better. I spoke to BFATT and my parents about struggling with them and keeping positive whilst doing them alone, and we said each day we would do a few exercises together, but I HAD to start doing them alone too. I did, I stopped lying and I did these exercises; usually in the morning or at night whilst crying.

Giving up sucks. When I was in the ICU, I had given up many times, those around me fought so incredibly hard to keep me alive and yet here I was again wanting to give up. Wanting everything that was taken from me to be handed back over to me again, but unfortunately that isn't how life works.

I am here, I didn't give up. For those of you who stuck by me and constantly nagged me, thank you. For those of you who dealt with the days where I felt low, thank you for bringing me back up again. YOU are the reason I kept going, you are the reason that now I will not give up. I learnt the hard way that giving up will get you nowhere, this stroke will not beat me.

People often say to me how positive I always am, some of you often joke and ask if I ever get sad. The answer is yes, of course I get sad but as you can see from reading my story, I hit my all-time lows battling through cancer, pneumonia, and a stroke. So yes, whilst I remain positive as much as I can, I still have days where I feel low, but these days are rare, however when they come it's explosive and unbearable because I am an ugly crier. Yup some of you guys know when I cry it is gross and so long. I often in my snotty state wonder

when the hell the tears will end!
I just think you are allowed to feel whatever emotion you need to feel, especially if you are going through cancer, pneumonia, a stroke, or ANYTHING you don't even need to be suffering from an illness YOU can feel how the hell you want to feel okay? If you are tired and need a break, take it, if you are fed up with something, write it down or talk to someone to vent. I have gone through so many emotions during the entire time from 2006 right up until this very day and it is okay to not be okay. I spent a long-time bottling stuff up. There is a limit to how much you can keep in, you don't need to shout to the world that you are struggling (if you are) you do however need to try and reach out to someone. I have so many lovely friends and I will often go to them about different things if I need to. I know my family are always there if I need them, but my friends are usually my go-to for any venting I have.
What I learnt from all of this is that I know in myself when I am run down and I am comfortable enough to tell people I just need the day, or however long it may be. I am grateful that my closest friends will allow this but not for too long, because it's not healthy. If you completely close off, it is hard to open back up to people again. Whilst I was in ICU after the stroke, I closed off unintentionally to everyone and then as I got better it became intentional and harder and harder to see people. It isn't that I DIDN'T want to see them, it is because it had been so long that I felt too distant to feel like I was able to and it caused anxiety, which many of you probably suffer from too. You need to know your limits. If you know me, you'll know I'm a little social butterfly and I freak out if I go a week without meeting up with friends or doing something, anything. For example, my friends Stu and Luke were trying to find a weekend where I was free so we could grab some beers and hang out. I recall them both saying something along the lines of "we are going to book you in now before you get too busy for us. Haha."

They asked me in early January of that year...and my response was "ummm not kidding guys, my next free weekend is early June."

JUNE.

Something I have recently done is to start giving myself a whole weekend or at least a day in which I see no one and there are no commitments. I hate letting people down and I always would rather it drain me and wear me down more than let someone else down. This has changed, because it had to and because I am no fun or use to anyone when I'm run down. Also, we need to look after ourselves! We need to look after ourselves and each other. If you know someone is struggling, reach out to them or if you haven't heard from someone in a short while ask them how they are.

How are you?

Fine.

I would ALWAYS say I was "fine" even for a few years after being ill. 'Fine' because does anyone care? Do you actually want me to answer that truthfully or are you asking out of politeness? Now when people ask that question, they know that they will either be faced with "yeah sweet" which is similar to fine but these days I mean I actually am fine...or they get a short story response on how I am feeling...so they better be ready for it. They usually are ready for my responses, check in on your friends and loved one's guys. Those three simple words can make someone's day. For me and it won't work for everyone as you need to find ways that work for you, is to write. I find writing helps my mood and this book despite it bringing up the past which many of you say must be hard to 'drag up' bad memories from the past has been incredible. I will never forget I fought against

Cancer, Pneumonia, and a Stroke but even though it was in 2006 there are still everyday battles that I face. By writing I don't mean you need to start writing a book, it could be that you write in a diary, and it doesn't need to be an essay, it could just be how you are feeling in that moment, just a few words.

Reading is a great escape too so if you are reading this thanks for choosing my words for your day. Some of my favourite reads: **The Lord Of The Rings & The Hobbit** by J. R. R. Tolkien (yeah...I had a lot of time during treatment to read these okay! They are also incredible, but watch the films if you prefer), **On The Road** by Jack Kerouac and **Into The Wild** by Jon Krakauer.

I could probably list a few more but if there is anything you should read it should be this one **The Diving-Bell and the Butterfly** by Jean-Dominique Bauby my friend Sandee told me about this book, and I love it so much. Jean-Dominique Bauby suffered from a stroke which left him with locked-in syndrome, the ENTIRE book was written by him blinking his left eyelid, it took ten months for it to finalise with over 200,000 blinks. It is the most beautiful thing I have ever read and the most interesting thing you might ever read. There is also a film if you aren't into reading, but I do BEG that you read it first. I read it in a few hours and have read it about 10 times. As you can imagine it isn't the biggest book ever...but it will have a huge impact. I can relate to it a lot, that feeling of feeling trapped in your body after a stroke is so well represented in the movie.

Which brings me onto one of my favourite escapes: MUSIC. Listen to whatever you fancy, during lockdown I set my drumkit back up. I couldn't play very long at all, maybe 5 minutes…by the end of lockdown it was a lot longer but nowhere like how I used to be able to play. Music has an escape like no other, it can bring every single emotion within minutes. You can smile, laugh, cry, and reminisce. It's the best. Okay music & exercise are my favourite ways to escape.

Combined or separately. I love running and I love the outdoors. Walking, running, any exercise, fresh air. All of it. Instant happiness.

There is something really beautiful about music, there is a song to suit your every mood and there will just be a moment when you hear a song and it stays with you forever, and that is just an incredible feeling.

I hated having CT scans and MRI scans. I had several of these scans, but the MRI scan is like having your head in a washing machine filled with screws and nails, it is LOUD. They often would play a cd of my choice through the headphones that you had to wear during the MRI scan, and this just made it so much more bearable. I love music. Nothing beats it and there is always a certain song that just hits you. Or several songs, I cannot express how great music is. So, if it is your go-to for escaping and chilling, I am there with you!

I love chilling but it has taken me a LONG time to work out this balance and to allow myself to not feel bad for relaxing.

I am currently listening to Sam Brookes. If you want to and I think you should always be open to listening to new music, give him a little listen.

I first heard of Sam through a band called The Volt that he used to be a part of, I saw them way back in 2008 at Glastonbury where I met one my best friends and "cancer" friend Ali Peart.

CHAPTER 15

ALI

Ali, my dearest, beautiful, and strongest friend ever. These words will never justify your greatness. I dedicate my entire book to you. I was so lucky to have been a part of your life. I met Ali in 2008 at Glastonbury festival where this photo was taken. I was lucky enough to go with a cancer charity called CLIC Sargent (as they were known at the time, now "Young Lives vs Cancer") with a bunch of other awesome people who were recovering from cancer or still going through treatment.

Everyone travelled together on a minibus from Bristol to Glastonbury with a few pickups on the way. None of us knew each other, we were all strangers to one another. I knew Phil from before I was ill, he used to manage the band The Volt that I mentioned previously and Sam Brookes for a while. Phil was the Music Coordinator for CLIC Sargent.

I remember after one of the pickups hearing an amazing accent. I turned around and looked at the girl and asked if she was Canadian. She laughed and said yes, she laughed because she said often people thought she was American. She had a wicked laugh, and I mean that in the best way. You know when someone just has such an infectious laugh or presence that you just want to know more about them? Well, I don't know about you, but I love meeting new people and I knew in seconds that there was something pretty cool about her.

Everyone else joined in with the conversations and all these strangers became a small family to me and to each other for the Glasto weekend. This was the first time and the longest I had been away from home by myself, but I wasn't scared. CLIC Sargent have the most incredible team. I mean I was nervous in the very beginning because I had never gone away with a bunch of people that I had never met before, but it is one of my all-time favourite memories and I will be forever glad that I went.

All we had to do was pack our bags and bring spending money, when we arrived on site the team from CLIC Sargent already had huge tents set up for us in the best location possible, near everything we would need for our stay. All the girls stayed on one side of the tent and the boys stayed in another part. The tent was so huge it was like a little house.

We were lucky enough to camp VIP behind the John Peel stage. This meant we had access to warm showers, and shortcuts behind the stages to get better access to the rest of the site without having to be pushed through the thousands of people. It also meant we had priority viewing spots (sometimes on the side of the stage) dotted around the site if we needed them. I discovered so much incredible music new and old, as well as meeting what would become one of my best friends. Now I am lucky enough to have some incredible friends in my life and all very close ones too. If you haven't got a chapter in my book, it isn't because I value you any less…I don't think there would even be enough pages in the world to justify you all.

Me and Ali couldn't stop talking when we met, we had so much in common and one thing that always stuck with me was her obsession with James Morrison, she LOVED the guy. We spoke about where she lived in Portsmouth, she spoke about her Mum Carole and her brothers Aaron and Julian. Not forgetting the best part, her dog Logan...who she had named after Wolverine in X-Men. Now if you guys know me well, you'll know I love Marvel and so this was all awesome stuff. We geeked out about X-Men for a bit and spoke endlessly about all kinds of stuff.

We all had a wicked time at Glastonbury. I was so happy, I loved meeting all these new people and I loved being able to be surrounded by people that I could relate to. I felt the most normal being around them because I didn't feel alone. Not all of us discussed our illnesses with each other to a huge depth as this was just an escape from it all, but we had all spoken about the stages we were at, and I think it was only myself and a few others that were finished with treatment.

Ali kept talking to me about Terry. I was like who the heck is Terry? Is he, her boyfriend? So, guys, Terry was her brain tumour. Terry the tumour, he had a few names, Tiny Tim was his name after radiation and if he had shrunk in size, but Terry is the one I remember the most. I never thought much about it, I just thought cool nice to meet you Terry, but you don't sound like much fun. Much like when I was told what form of cancer I had; I didn't have a clue what it meant. After Ali told me that she had a brain tumour she thanked me, I asked why she did, and she said because I didn't treat her any differently or react weirdly once she told me. Why would I? I got that completely, man did I understand. The word cancer or tumour, the connotations that come along with it are so exhausting, that I understood why she thanked me. Now I had never known anyone with a brain tumour before, nor did I know anything about it. What I did know is there was Ali, my friend, and Terry the Tumour. I didn't need to know anything else. I thought it was great that she named it and it made me laugh. She would often say 'fuck Terry' or that he was a prick, and we would just laugh about it. We danced to Jay Z, we met some incredible bands backstage all over the weekend that CLIC had arranged for us. My favourite moment was meeting Richard Ashcroft from The Verve, he was incredibly lovely. He spent so much time with us all and declined interviews with the press to spend more time talking to us. Me and Ali had dry lips and he heard Ali mention it, so he asked his PA to go and get her some Vaseline, what an absolute legend.

Me and Ali kept in contact after meeting at Glastonbury. We would text, Facebook, email, call each other but I also visited her in Portsmouth as much as I could, and I loved my train journeys to her. She would meet me at the station, and we would hang out with her Mum, go shopping or chill and watch Bad Boys the movie.

The reason I usually went to Portsmouth instead of her coming to Bristol was that she was often in and out of appointments so needed to be near her hospital. I didn't care at all about me going there, if anything I loved it as it boosted my confidence as I was still struggling with adapting to life after the stroke and so this tiny bit of independent travelling helped me a ton and Ali never realised how much it helped me. I often went with her to appointments if she had any during my visits. We mainly hung out at her home with Logan, ("Logie Bear" as Ali called him) drank at a place called 'The Reg', ate junk food and watched movies. Her Mum Carole was always so lovely to me, it felt like my second home. Then over time I met more of her family, and they all made me feel so welcome that I felt like I was part of their family bubble.

She came to Bristol a handful of times as her brother Julian lived here for a few years. I got to meet both of her brothers who are lush. They are such a remarkable family. Each one of them is so kind and caring, and an absolute pleasure to know. Her friends back in Portsmouth were awesome, I got to meet a bunch of them, and they were all so friendly almost like you'd known them for years. I'll never forget the first time Ali introduced me to her friends and it always baffled me. She wouldn't say "Hey guys, this is Leena." She would say "Hey guys, this is my cancer friend...Leena." It always threw me, especially the very first time she said it, I wasn't expecting it. Then I thought you know what, the reason we met is yes because I had cancer and she **has** cancer. If this is her way of dealing with it and if this is how she wants to introduce me then you do what you gotta do. The reason it was a shock initially is because I tried quite often to never let people know what I had been through in those early years, especially new people because it freaked me out. I didn't ever want to put people in an awkward position, and I never quite wanted the reactions I would receive.

All my friends are incredible, and you guys know that, but meeting someone that could relate to the numerous scans, the endless amount of blood tests, the sleepless nights, the side effects, the needles, or just to sit in silence with each other and know that the person next to you feels exactly the same. Now I am not saying what I had was anywhere near as hard as Ali had it, she always thought it was amazing what I had battled and been through. I would sit there and think you need to look in the mirror because you my friend are the bravest thing that walked this planet. There is no friend like a cancer friend, Ali was my first cancer friend and I have never felt more honored for her to call me that. The way she said it so freely and with such ease made me realise she was a strong person, most definitely stronger than me and the strongest person I will ever know. When I started working in a Boots store here in Bristol, it turned out that one of Ali's best mates from Portsmouth worked there too – Ollie. He was studying in Bristol, and it was so cool that we had even more of a connection, what a crazy small world. When Ali was in Bristol, we would meet up with Ollie too. Me and Ali always said we would try and go visit her brother Aaron in Whistler together. Ali often went back to Canada for holidays and to visit her family, her Dad Bruce lives out there and so she often went back when she was able to. I had always wanted to go to Canada, and it had always been on the top of my list for a very long time, unfortunately we never got to go together.

The last time I saw Ali in Portsmouth was January 2012 during a visit to her doctor. I waited in the waiting room until her and Carole had finished, but they called me into the room. Ali had asked her Mum to come and get me as she wanted me to be there to hear what they had to say.

I went into the room with Carole and was told then and there how much time she had left to live. Me and Carole were in a worse state than Ali. From the moment I met Ali, I never once thought to myself that she wouldn't survive this. I never researched it, I never asked her if it was curable, it just never crossed my mind. We just hung out as friends do but as time went on you could see the damage Terry was causing her and the result of the pressure Terry was having against her brain. Her eyesight got worse and countless other side effects but I never for a moment saw anything than my beautiful friend Ali. Beautiful through and through, there is no one like her in this world and I will never find anyone that could compare to her beauty and strength. I never cared that she looked different every time I saw her, which made me realise that my friends when I was ill really didn't care about how I looked either; I suddenly understood it all. I hated going into hospitals with her because I spent so much time in them myself, but it wasn't about me, and I never told Ali. Carole knew I found it hard, but I didn't want Ali to know, it was about her, and I would do it over and over a thousand times more.

I never thought about the harsh reality that of course Terry could kill her, Terry you prick.

Turns out it was Ali comforting me. It takes a lot to hear such devastating news, but it takes a beautiful and inspiring person to handle it so gracefully.

The timescale she was given is not one I want to discuss because I am trying my best to portray her the best I can because she meant an awful lot to me, but I also do not want to upset her family or friends because this is not the intention of my story. What I will say is that I had train tickets to go and see her in early May 2012, so did Ollie. She was planning a birthday party in Portsmouth, and we were all so excited. She threw a decent party!

Me and Ollie never got on that train together, she passed away two days after her 22nd birthday and the next train me and Ollie got together was to her funeral. It was nice talking to Ollie on the train about our memories of her, and what an impact she had on us all. We cried, laughed, smiled, and sat in silence during the train journey from Bristol to Portsmouth. It broke my heart to come to the reality that I would never see her again, but her service was stunning. Logan her dog was there, and it was full of people that loved Ali. It was packed, the entire room was full, and it was incredibly beautiful and colourful. Ali had said to her Mum that she didn't want anyone to wear black to her funeral as she thought it was such a depressive colour. She wanted people to celebrate the life that she lived and not to be sad. I loved that about her, even knowing what was to come she still wanted those of us to be brightly dressed and not to feel sorrow. She had many touching songs playing during her funeral, which she had helped select, but the one that broke me and left me uncontrollably crying the entire time was a song by James Morrison.

I listened to this song constantly for quite some time as it made me feel close to her again, yet I realised how punishing this was to myself. I never listened to it again until a work colleague told me what her song would be for her first dance. She played it to me at work and boy did it hit a nerve. When that wedding came and I heard that song again it broke me, so I watched the newlyweds dance for a few moments before escaping and heading to the bar.

I don't want this to be a sad chapter because yes of course it is, sad would be an understatement but she brought so much happiness into my life and into the world that I don't want it to be sad. It broke my heart when I received a phone call about her passing. I will never forget that morning; I had never lost a friend before and losing Ali tore me apart. To lose someone with whom you connected so easily, because you were each other's "cancer" friend, sucked. She knew that she wouldn't survive this disease and even knowing that she simply smiled and made me laugh. I know it was an honour to know her. Loss is a bizarre thing which I guess all of us unfortunately experience during our lifetime. Each of us will go through the same emotions but we will each take whatever amount of time it needs to take to heal. It doesn't mean that you "get over it", it just means you learn to live with it and grow stronger. You cry less and less and start to smile at the memories and focus on the good times that you were able to share. The first few days in May will always be hard because she was special, and I miss her. There are many similarities I see in her family and so to still speak to them or to hear them laugh is often like hearing Ali laugh. She was so incredible that she never once made you feel sorry for her, not once.

She just woke up and got on with her day, and I always loved her for that. Some people often referred to her as a trooper, and yes, she was.
Alexandra Peart, I love you now and always. Thank you for being you, thank you for not giving a shit for what others thought and for reminding me who I really was and for helping me feel me again.
Thank you for making such a huge impact on my life and for having me as your cancer friend. Thank you for saying you would keep in touch as often people say but thank you for actually doing it. Those 4 years I had you in my life were the most incredible and I will forever cherish those memories.

May you shine on in Whistler after putting up the most extraordinary battle and may you finally rest in peace.

I made it to Canada mate, most importantly I met up with your bro Aaron and we enjoyed some beers with the best view – looking out at you!

CHAPTER 16

AIMEE

Aimee! Captain B, Mrs. Holmes to be! Whatever you might call her; Aimee, I love you and I thank you for getting me through things you probably never realised you got me through; and for being there for me no matter where you are in the world.

I met this weirdo at Beach Break Live festival in 2010. Now I never would have met her if it wasn't for Ali. After meeting Ali at Glastonbury in 2008, we kept in touch. Ali had told me that she was going to a festival with CLIC Sargent again, they had a spot left and would I be interested in going, HECK YES.

Music, as I mentioned before, is just incredible, the way it can bring people together is just the best. Cancer brought me two of the greatest friends I have ever had. Cancer brought many bad things but the good things that it brought made it all worthwhile. It gave me a chance to meet the strongest person I have ever come across in this world – Ali Peart and without Ali I never would have met Aimee. Ali went back with CLIC Sargent to Glastonbury in 2009, a year after we met. On a visit to Ali in Portsmouth she spoke about all the incredible people she had met. I remember her saying she had met someone called Aimee and that she'd think we'd get along. I remember meeting Aimee and thought she looked super cool, she had this awesome t-shirt on with photos of her and her boyfriend (soon to be husband!) on that he had made for her (Craig, alright lad?) The group of people that went to Beach Break were awesome, we all got along so well but there was something about Aimee that I just loved, her attitude and her laugh just made me think I want this person in my life. Without sounding too cheesy, you just know when you've met a good egg don't you? Ali was right. I did get along with her. We all had such a laugh at this festival, alongside Glastonbury 2008, Beach Break Live 2010 is one memory that I hold very close to my heart.

We met some incredible bands backstage again (thanks CLIC!) Aimee borrowed one of my tops...I mean she couldn't have run out of clothes because she has an endless supply, but it looked better on her anyway. We all did some horse riding and an activity called 'Go Ape' where I discovered my fear of ladders. Aimee was really encouraging and helped me along the way, even when I thought *nope, I'm done!*

I am so happy that Ali asked me to go to this festival with her, and I am so glad that she introduced me to her other "cancer" friend Aimee. I was into photography, and I noticed Aimee had this awesome camera. So, we got talking about that for quite a bit over the weekend, it was Craig's, and she was scared to let anyone use it in case we broke it, haha. We spoke about her cancer and about her life in general back home in Barry. We all danced, drank, chilled (napped a lot in Aimee's case) and just had the best time. It always fascinated me how easily this girl managed to nap, at one point she passed out asleep during a DJ set backstage, I'm sure of it...if only there was evidence...

Aimee had the most positive and can-do personality, much like Ali. It wasn't until later on that I discovered how much Aimee had been through, yet even through such a tough time she smiled whilst telling me her story. Ali was right, Aimee was cool. Inside and out, and if you know me, you'll know I love dinosaurs and this kid has a dino bag – so what's not to like!?

Aimee you are such a kind and positive soul. Your laugh is infectious, and you never fail to make me smile. Your kindness, honesty and positivity are a beautiful thing to see, it never gets old. Keep being you. I feel lucky to have been able to meet you. Even luckier that we have both stayed in touch and are still friends today. I always believe that things in life happen for a reason. Me, Ali and Aimee all had different forms of cancer, and each had to fight through our own battles, yet without going through this we would never have met. After Ali passed away, I would message Aimee quite a bit and without realising she always managed to get me through the day. She may never have known how low I was feeling or that she was helping me, but she did, and I'll be forever grateful Aimee. So, thank you. Thank you for especially finding the time for me when we are often in different time zones and for always being there no matter what.

To have such amazing and incredible friends that you can rely on in life is awesome and I really feel lucky to have all of you in my life. Whilst I strongly stick by what I said in the last chapter that no one could ever compare to Ali, no two people could ever be compared as we are all different.

However, we all have similar traits and that is what bonds people, builds friendships and relationships. Me and Aimee both lost Ali amongst many other people that loved her, but we also had such a great time when we all met, and I know from stories Ali told me when she and Aimee met in 2009 that they made some wicked memories too.

These memories and moments in time are priceless and should never be taken for granted. I know Aimee has also lost people to the big 'C' and so have many of you guys reading this. We both lost a close friend of ours called Steve who was such a cool guy and always there to help you or make you laugh. Steve, we love you and hope you are shining brightly wherever you are.

It is such a crazy thing to go through cancer, but you can meet some incredible people during such a hard time, and it only keeps you going and staying positive. You help each

other through these moments and become stronger within yourselves. When you have been through so much it opens your eyes and makes you appreciate what you have and makes you see the world in a completely different light.
Aimee and her soon to be husband Craig are two of the most genuine and kindest souls that you will ever meet. Down to earth, hilarious and want to achieve the best that they can, and they do. Which is the most important thing, right? To go through something and to now appreciate each new day means that we are lucky. We live on for those who are no longer with us, we live on and live the best lives that we can because we are able to. Craig and Aimee most certainly live their best lives and rule their own worlds, both unique and inspiring and two of the nicest people you will ever come across.
Thank you both for coming to Bristol and celebrating my 10-year Cancerversary with me and my other friends despite how busy you guys are, it meant the world. Aimee thank you again for everything, for being a friend to Ali and for being there for me still today. Love you mate!

PS – I need to join you somewhere around the world soon for sure.

CHAPTER 17

PHIL

Phil works for or at the time of meeting him worked for CLIC Sargent. I have met some of the most amazing people through this charity, they have brought some incredible people into my life including two of my closest friends. They supported me and my family whilst I was getting my life back on track, they kept in contact when I was healthy and still to this day, I speak to some of the greats that work (or worked) for them (Hi Sally! Hi Jeremy!)

I mentioned the legend that is Phil Day earlier in this book. It is because of you Phil that I ever had the chance for Ali to be in my life, and though it was only four years, it was the most incredible four years I ever had until she was able to finally rest in peace. Thank you for your support at her funeral, and for keeping my head up high and passing me all the tissues necessary. Without you I never would have met her and without her I never would have met Aimee. You and CLIC Sargent have made a huge impact on my life, and I will be forever grateful.

As I mentioned previously, I was in a band before I was diagnosed and me and my best friend Sophie often went to a few local gigs.

When we were 15, we would help local bands with their

mailing list and just hang out with the bands because we were cool (at least that's what we tell ourselves...however I stand by the fact that we are and were cool).

Phil used to manage a few of these bands and whilst I was going through treatment Soph mentioned that Phil worked for CLIC Sargent and put me in contact with him. It wasn't until a few months down the line after the stroke that I contacted Phil. I hadn't heard of this charity until that moment. CLIC helped fund a laptop for me later down the line whilst I got back into studying. I was diagnosed during my A-Levels and so I never managed to complete them, but I was keen to study again. I eventually ended up doing a Foundation Degree in Photography and the money towards a laptop helped me so much.

As I was 18 when I was diagnosed, I seemed to slip through the cracks as it were, as other people my age or younger seemed to know of all these charities and all had a lot of help during their treatments. I did have help from people but as I wasn't on a children's ward, I kind of felt a bit forgotten. Also, there were times I was just too ill and so out of it I might have had people come in to visit me and I might have slept through their visits.

Most of my help came after, once I was discharged but I wouldn't change it for the world because had I discovered them sooner, I may never have met the incredible people I knew or now know.

If you are reading this and perhaps fall into the "Adult" category, or a 'Young Adult' being between 16-24 years of age I would highly recommend seeking out this charity. They are now called Young Lives VS Cancer. They can help in ways beyond what I could list. They offer home from homes so you can have your family nearby whilst you are in hospital, they are incredible. I'm not saying that you are left alone if you are 18 but when I was diagnosed it felt a lot different to other people's experiences. I would really urge you to seek what help there might be out there for you during such a hard time, especially if you are classed as an adult. I found it hard when I was 18 and I would hope that now after so many years passing that these charities are more accessible to you, no matter what age you may be when you or your loved ones are affected. My sister Vicky actually worked in one of CLIC Sargent's Home from Homes, so I got a chance to visit the one that she worked in, and it is incredible. Filled with hope and care, it really feels like a home for the families that need it.

There are so many people out there who can help you through, but CLIC Sargent were absolute heroes to me. I didn't know how much I needed their help until I got it. Through meeting all the amazing people that work with them and from going to so many events with them it slowly built my confidence back up and I was becoming more 'me' again. Phil was the music coordinator for CLIC and through him and the charity I was able to go to Glastonbury Festival in 2008 and Beach Break Live Festival in 2010. I met some astonishing people, met more people that worked for CLIC, made more incredible friends, camped VIP and met numerous artists backstage at each of these festivals. Though it is not visible to you unless you know my backstory with how the stroke affected my life, CLIC were aware and not once did they forget during my times away with them. Be it carrying my bags, carrying my food, cutting food for me, or simply just checking in on me. They do it with such care, compassion and it is a blessing to be anyone that works for this charity because you all absolutely make a huge difference to anyone that is ill and made a huge difference to my life.

As well as the two festivals that I was lucky enough to be a part of, Phil knew I was trying to get back into photography and so he invited me along to two music workshops that CLIC Sargent were doing.

The first one was in 2013 at a beautiful location called Grittleton Place, one of the bands I used to love before I fell ill was a band called Blackbud. The band at this point had parted ways but their bassist Adam Newton and drummer Sam Nadel were both mentors on this course, so it was nice to see familiar faces. I brought my drum kit along to this workshop for everyone to use for the duration of the course. It made me sad for a few moments to see others play it when I was unable to play anymore. Yet I would smile because music just has such an amazing power that you can't help but feel every single emotion when you are surrounded by it.

Sam Nadel thank you for getting me to pick those drumsticks back up even if only for a few minutes. You are an incredible drummer and spending time that week watching you teach, watching you drum and have a jam with Adam just brought a smile to my face, it made me want to try and drum again.

Another course was the Hot House Festival in 2014. Here I bumped into Sam Brookes. He was one of the mentors on this course, there were several musicians running these courses and I was there to document them throughout the week. Simon Whitehead was the videographer at both of these events, and I was there to offer any help, to look over at how he worked and to take some stills of everything coming together.

The aim of these workshops was to bring young people affected by cancer together and for them all to work with each other throughout the week to create songs. At the end of the week, they would showcase their collaborations in a performance. It was a great way to meet people, to see other young adults going through something so traumatic but to see them smile was so nice, and I can only imagine how rewarding that must be for this charity.

They were all so happy in this space that CLIC had provided them. I felt very lucky to be a part of these courses too. So many incredible mentors, singers, songwriters, composers, vocalists, drummers, guitarists etc you name it, these rooms had it.

As well as documenting these events I had always wanted to give something back to the charity, even if something small.

I did a 5k with my sister to help raise money for them, took part in a 'no-make up selfie' campaign on their social media and set up a little stall one Christmas with my sister in Bristol to help fundraise for them too.

CLIC Sargent – to ALL of you, however you are involved, thank you. You make the world an easier place to live in whilst going through cancer, even after you have finished treatment. The care that every single one of you brings to others is remarkable and you are the best.

Whilst I was getting back into work and struggling with job applications CLIC helped me constantly. I even got to help volunteer in their warehouse here in Bristol. I was taking photos of things to sell through their eBay site. This meant I was picking my camera back up again and meant I was able to fill a huge gap on my CV which was there due to being ill for so long.

Thank you for allowing me to help and for giving me a chance when not many others would. Thank you for boosting my confidence when I was knocked down repeatedly. For making me laugh, smile, and cry but for all the right reasons. For bringing back old faces from bands that I never thought I would come across again, to meeting the bands at Glastonbury and Beach Break Live whom I have loved for so long. For listening to my journey and for not judging a single word I said. For supporting my family, through supporting me. For being such incredible and approachable individuals that I know you are there if I ever need you. Thank you for doing what you do and for making everyone's lives all that bit easier, and for bringing joy when there is often so much doubt.

For bringing joy, when even though the journey for some may be coming to an end; but for being absolute heroes anyway until the last moment. CLIC Sargent – I love you guys and I thank you.

CHAPTER 18

LIFE AFTER THE STROKE

Life after a stroke is crazy, it's basically like a second life, a second chance at life which yeah in my case it was. No one can prepare you mentally for how you will deal with it and not even your own brain knows what the heck is going on either, so you are basically doomed.

Or are you?

That is what it might feel like for quite some time and it isn't easy but there are some better days to come, I promise you. With all the times in and out of hospitals over 5 years, all the physio sessions and trying each day to be understood and heard, was hard. I'm not going to lie to you, it is hard. Then if it was easy, what's the point?
To have everything taken away from you just like that after battling so hard to get through cancer SUCKED, like give me a break. However, having a stroke taught me so much. As if I hadn't already learnt enough from having cancer, the world just thought they'd throw in pneumonia and a stroke too. Don't feel sorry for me, I don't want that...but work with me here. Without it I wouldn't be who I am today. Without it I wouldn't appreciate each day and I wouldn't know what

it is to work hard to recover and become more me again. You discover so much about yourself going through these devastating things, or anything hard that you might come across in life, it may not be cancer or a stroke. For me it was cancer, pneumonia, stroke, grief...you name it I tackled it. The highs and lows make you stronger, even the lows. You just learn to pick yourself back up again, time after time.

What you aren't prepared for is "normal" life after a stroke, because the chances are you haven't fully recovered, are still recovering or have to take each day as it comes and learn how to adapt to this "new you", which by the way is incredible – you rule.

For me, it was hard. I had a lot to deal with and I wasn't sure if at the beginning I would ever talk again or walk again but I got there, believe me it was hard work to say the least and the hard work just kept on coming. Once I was able to speak again and walk, I was then able to be a lot more independent, however there were struggles and obstacles that got in the way, but I didn't want to be stuck inside forever. I wanted to start having a normal life again, as normal as can be for me anyway. I wanted to start getting back into work and was completely terrified of the idea all at the same time. By this point I hadn't worked in two years, not because I didn't want to but because 10 months of that was spent in hospitals and then the rest of that was building myself back up again to talk, walk and be able to look after myself again. When I was eventually ready to start looking for work, I had to think really hard about what I could and couldn't do, then my family made a very good point – companies shouldn't focus on any disabilities, but my abilities. That made me feel more confident in applying, but I tell you now back then it was a lot of application forms, so not only was my writing unreadable due to it being my non-dominant hand that was filling them in; it also took hours per form. I wasn't fussy at all about where I was applying to, I just wanted to start getting my life back on track again and start having a routine that wasn't just hospital visits and counting to ten. I kid you not when I tell you I applied to EVERY single shop in The Galleries Shopping Centre Broadmead here in Bristol in 2008 (many of the shops are gone now), and there is that little box you can tick if you consider yourself to have a disability, sometimes I ticked it, often I didn't. I wasn't sure if they would judge me differently and disregard the application if I had ticked it, then I also questioned whether or not to tick that box because I didn't want to have more of a chance than others just because I had a weakness in my right arm and hand. A lot went on in my brain during this time and believe me there were MONTHS of applying to places everywhere and anywhere.

I didn't hear back from anyone, I started to feel disheartened and felt very low during this time. I had spent so long to build myself back up and to feel more independent, that I had forgotten in life what rejection was. I had battled more than enough, now they were starting all over again. Life is one continuous gamble and there are always going to be things knocking you back, but you get up and you knock back harder, that's it – punch em! I'm kidding, please don't hit anyone. I don't condone violence. I will NEVER forget this one interview I had at Julian Graves. I was SO excited that finally a company had got back to me and wanted to see ME. Now this shop is similar to Holland and Barrett, a health food shop of the sort. I felt nervous and thought how much I wanted this job so much to be able to say I am one step closer to normality, in your face stroke. I couldn't have been more wrong, this interview threw me and to a place where I feel I was at the start of all this – low, worried, and scared. I cannot remember her name, but I do remember thinking that I wanted to walk out before I had even sat down. The formality of the interview was standard, I introduced myself, we shook hands (which by the way isn't something I like doing because it doesn't always happen and you'll end up shaking my fist or I am unable to tell my brain to let go of your hand…awkward.) So anyway, I stated who I was, she shook my hand, thumb included, and we walked over to the interview room. *Deep breaths here* I thought, *deep breaths*. We spoke a bit about the hours and about the job itself but then she asked me something, I'll never forget it.

"So, I see you have ticked the box that says you have a disability, tell me more about that and how it will be a problem?"

Now I didn't mind talking about it, but everything that followed this question was incredibly demeaning and a waste of time. She would say that deliveries get made to the other end of the shopping centre and how well do I think I would cope or how would I stack the shelves. It went on, it was 20 minutes of push backs that I didn't need. I do not know if this company is still around, nor do I care. I hope this woman realised that her actions were completely unacceptable and instead of focusing on what I may or may not be able to do, her and the company perhaps should have focused on ways they could help or adapt to help me if I were to be successful in this role.

It goes without saying I didn't get the job, my response to "how will you push the trolley cage to the store with limited movement?" "Slowly probably, maybe slower than the other members of staff. If it means I need to come in earlier to get a job done then that is what I will do", got me nowhere. I didn't want to work for a company that could only see my weakness, whereas I see my weakness as a need to WANT to work harder and to try to achieve things even if they may not be achievable in a "normal" way.

This interview destroyed me in ways I cannot even express. I held it together until I got home, my Mum and Dad were not at all pleased with what I told them. They wanted to make a complaint, I told them not to and that maybe this is something I will come across more than once. I told them not to waste their time. I took a break from applying to anything for a short while because this really knocked me down.

After more application forms, CVs and emails I thought I was perhaps being ignored as my CV had a huge gap on it and no explanation. I did not want to write "there is a gap in my CV as I was in and out of hospital for a long time" because I didn't want that to define me, I would of course talk about it in interviews if it was required to do so but I didn't see the point mentioning it before that stage.

I ended up volunteering for CLIC Sargent in their Bristol Warehouse in May 2008. My job here was to photograph items for their e-bay site and I loved it! I loved meeting new people, and I loved the fact I was able to use a camera again, what's better is no one judged me, and I was able to work at my own pace and they asked if I needed help, they asked and they provided me with it, should I have needed it.

I had a phone call from Boots asking me to come in for an interview. I was excited but even more scared this time as I had ticked that disability box on this one too. I just thought I know to just walk out this time if things start looking ridiculous again.

The lovely woman who held the interview was called Angela, and she is a complete delight and a credit to the company. The interview was long, but we laughed in between, it felt so relaxed, and I felt comfortable, which was the complete opposite to the other interview I had. It came to the time in the interview where Angela wanted to know more about my disability. I was scared but she asked in such a genuine and caring way that I was excited to tell her. What made it even better was that she asked what they could do as a company to help me if I were to be successful.

I was told later that day that I was successful and that they really loved my can-do attitude. I GOT A JOB! AHHH. This was such a huge step and I was super excited, scared and petrified at the same time but this was it…I was finally piecing my life back together! When I started, we discussed what I would be comfortable doing. They asked if there were any areas of the store that I would like to work in but have perhaps not considered due to my weakness in my right arm. I cannot express how great this company was to work for and how amazing the staff were in helping me along the way. Thank you, Angela, for giving me a job when I felt like no one wanted me, it really helped me get my life back on track. Now, my main job was to be on the main tills and then later I worked on the fragrance department and helped on the No7 makeup counter (I know haha, me and makeup aren't the best of friends...I didn't ever put anything on anyone's face as they would look like a clown, I was just there to help customers find things.) I had voiced to Angela that I was concerned about being on the tills as I had no idea how I would pack away customers items, scan items and handle money. There was A LOT to think about and consider. At the start I would bag items for other members of the team whilst I was training, but when training was complete and I had to fly solo, it was challenging. Both physically and mentally.

Luckily the main tills had scanners that rested in place and so didn't need manual operation, however at times it wouldn't scan so I would have to place the item with the barcode facing up and reach over with my left hand to scan the item. Which was fine if it was a flat object, if it was shampoo, I was doomed as it would roll about, or I would have to wedge it in the corner before I could scan it. Most of the time these things went unnoticed, but what was evident is that I was very slow at serving customers. However, if I needed to go to the food tills, these scanners required a press of a button which only my left hand could do. I started wearing a wrist splint to work because customers' impatience and weird looks at how I did things started to take its toll.

With a wrist splint on, it was visible to the public that there was a reason behind my weird adaptive ways, and it seemed to help, and customers would start helping bag up too. I once served a lady and it took 40 minutes, she had several baskets, and it took ages to bag stuff up with one hand. It took so long, and she was so rude at how slow I was that members of staff came off their tills to help me. What would take minutes to most, took an eternity for me. When it came to payment, I prayed that everyone would pay by card, but of course this wasn't the case. When money was introduced, I would always drop it. I would have to place money onto the counter to count out what they had handed me, or worse when I was giving change, I would have to slide it back to them on the counter, which just felt so rude. Over time these things became easier, and I was able to work at a pace that I was happy with and customers were soon happy that I wasn't dumping their change on the counter or taking 20 minutes to scan one item. To all the staff at this Boots store thank you for your kindness, your help, and your patience throughout whilst I learnt ways in which I had to adapt to be able to do this job.

Thank you, Angela, Debs, Jayne, Ollie, Rhiannon, Kristina, Louise, Jess, Holly, Jan, Stacie, Joe, Carol, Sandra and anyone that worked on fragrance or within this store during my time there, you guys made it so much easier.

If you are reading this and are wondering how the heck you get your life back on track, you are doing it. By waking up each day and picking up that spoon you've dropped a thousand times or trying to count to 10 when you can only count to three, you will get there.

As I have said before no one has the same story, you may find this easier than I did and I may have had it easier than others but that doesn't mean it isn't hard for us, hard for you. From volunteering in May 2008 for CLIC Sargent and then to not being employed until 7 months later was a lot to handle. It may be that you are lucky and manage to find work quicker than I was able to, I am lucky in the sense that I was able to even work again. You may be sat reading this and your chances aren't looking so great, I was told by my family that they were told I wouldn't survive, and I did. Whatever your story, I am here for you, there are people there for you, please reach out and let them help you if help is what you need.

Life after a stroke is a never-ending battle but these battles become different each day and you will learn to love them. The obstacles that get in your way will be high, but they will lower, and you will be able to jump over them higher than the last. You will more than likely have days where things just don't look so good, but they will look better again, even if ever so slightly by that small percentage.

You will discover that you have come a long way and will discover that others will help you, or you will learn to find new ways to help yourself. It isn't going to be easy; it really isn't but with the help of those around you, you will get through this, let them help you because in doing so you are helping yourself. You may not be able to do things that perhaps you were able to do before and believe me when I say I know how frustrating and upsetting that is, and it isn't something you 'get over' it is just something you learn to be okay with and perhaps learn to adapt and learn new ways with this new version of you.

Life after a stroke is hard and it is filled with every single emotion. You are here, and you are alive, and I am here with you fighting through each day with you.

I am a cancer survivor, and I am a stroke survivor, and life after the stroke hasn't ended, I am still living with the impact it had on me still to this day.

I am so proud of myself to be where I am today, and I wouldn't have been able to do it without those of you in my life.

CHAPTER 19

MY LUCKY FIN

Just to make things easier for you all reading my book, and how I talk about my limbs…here is a little key!

My dominant hand: Right hand.
The hand affected after the stroke: Right hand.
My lucky fin: Right hand.
My non dominant hand, which is now my dominant hand and often referred to as my "good arm" or "good hand": Left hand/arm.

I have a lucky fin, I am nemo. I'm guessing most of you have probably seen the film 'Finding Nemo'? For those of you who haven't, Nemo is a clownfish, and he was born with one of his fins smaller than the other, he calls one of his fins his lucky fin. Coincidentally it is Nemo's right fin.
Most of you will more than likely be unaware of the daily battles or issues I still have; even to this very day, 17 years after I had the stroke. Even if you are my closest friends, it's sometimes forgotten, and I don't mean that in a bad way, if anything it's a good thing as it means I look or come across as "normal" to you.

When the stroke happened (or if you want to get technical the medical term is Cerebrovascular Accident or CVA), it affected the left side of my brain which caused paralysis on the right side of my body.
SO, where do I even begin? Right...if you are reading this try and spend an entire day only using your non-dominant hand, but your other hand cannot assist.
Try opening a new jar or something, your brain will more than likely naturally tell you to use both hands, especially if you are able to. For me it is a different story, of course things are easier now, but it doesn't mean that the little things I come across are much easier.
After the stroke I couldn't open a jar for months, maybe even years without help. There were times I would try and wedge it somewhere to try and open it, or hold it between my feet, or my knees, anywhere that I could grip and try and turn it with my left hand.
Today I still struggle, I have to place the jar into my right hand and position my fingers around it and try and keep it still whilst I twist the lid with my good hand. The issue here is that it often strains my right wrist as it is still weak and can cause a tiny bit of pain or discomfort. My sister Angel told me about grip mats which I have used for a few years now to open things, but sometimes it can take more than one attempt and I often have to rest in between so as not to strain my right wrist more than it can handle. Often, I won't notice if I have pushed it too much until much later as the reaction in my right arm and hand is often delayed, it varies day by day.
I once spent an hour trying to open a can of tuna, and yes before you suggest it – it was a **ring pull**. Tuna cans are particularly shorter than say a tin of beans, there isn't much to grip onto. Especially as all I can do with my right hand is open and close it, I am unable to tell my thumb to move out to the side or to lift each finger individually. The first initial part of a ring pull can is simple, but when you are unable to

grip it to fully pull the lid back, that's where things get frustrating. I usually end up wrapping my lucky fin in tea towels and trying to grip the tin without cutting myself.
YUP, I **once cut myself on a tuna lid.** I thought I would be smart and use my right hand to pull the lid back as I could then grip it with my good hand instead...NOPE. The right hand flung the sharp tuna lid uncontrollably into my left hand and cut my finger. After 20 minutes of trying to open this, it wasn't worth the blood covered tuna as a reward.
My parents bought me an electric can opener shortly after I was home from the stroke, and I was so upset and frustrated that this had to be bought that I made them take it back. I get that they were trying to help me, but I wanted to be able to try and use utensils normally. I didn't know that it would take up to an hour to open a can. I can use a standard can opener, but it often needs to be a specific one, or in general can take up to an hour for me to do. So, in the past month my parents have recently bought an electric can opener again...this time I didn't get upset or tell them to send it back, this time I used it.
Now, when I say I don't like to give up, for seventeen years I've struggled opening tins or cans (alongside many other things) …but I haven't given up, this sure as hell is a helpful thing to have in the house. Whenever people say to me do I think about giving up, or do I accept that I have reached my full recovery, yeah maybe I have...but give me that can opener and I'll give it another 17 years no problem. I do not accept that this is how I will be forever, because 17 years ago I couldn't cut my own food, feed myself, wash myself...so if it takes me this long to open a can, I just need to prep food ahead of time, it's not an issue, it's frustrating but it's just understanding and adapting to this new me. My lucky fin just takes a bit longer than most, but it's still lucky.
Enough about tuna, by the way…if I ever make you a meal, I promise you I'm OCD with hygiene and you won't have any blood in your food or parts of my hand in there, I

PROMISE!
Another problem that I face is **carrying things**, for example depending on the mug if I'm making cups of tea, it is very rare to be able to carry two at a time...so when you worked in an office and stupidly ask if your team wanted a drink, and they ALL said yes...it was mentally stressful and physically demanding. Now don't get me wrong I loved doing it, but it is a very **difficult** thing for me to do. When so many others offered to get you a drink, it's a natural reaction to want to get them one too. Also, I'm a nice person and I like to do these nice things, but I often spilt everyone's drinks on the way back or had a breakdown halfway back to the room because my brain was in overload thinking about carrying all of these, and more than likely my right arm is throbbing and wants me to drop that tray right that very minute, but I persevered.
If you are reading this and perhaps have made me 20 drinks in one week, then I shoot off and just make my own later on and don't offer to make you one...I'm not being rude, I'm just physically tired from that one time before. Needless to say, my colleagues were awesome and usually ran out of the room to take the tray and carry it for me, but I am also stubborn and when people offer to take it off me and carry it...I politely decline, then sit at the desk with a seriously achy arm the rest of the day.
Which leads me onto my next issue...**ROUNDS**. If I am out with my friends in the pub and we are all doing rounds, I usually hope and pray they all order something like a bottle of Peroni...because bottles are easier to carry than pints. Making several trips back and forth to the bar really isn't fun, but neither is having to explain WHY you are unable to carry more than one drink at a time, every time. I am SO lucky that the majority of my friends do know and will often help me carry them or I trust them with my debit card, and they just grab the next round for me. However, when it's new people it is a weird thing to have to explain and I'm not trying to get

myself out of buying the next round honest, I'm usually the one who has bought 4 rounds more than everyone else because I am stupidly kind, or you just haven't given my debit card back yet...I see you.

It is something that I admit I will try my best to avoid telling you because it is nice if you haven't noticed yet, or ever notice. Then again, if there are 12 of you it's going to be a hell of a wait whilst it is my round so, I'll end up having to explain eventually. I find the more I talk about it, yes it becomes easier to talk about, but everyone reacts differently, and I just want you to know that no reaction makes me feel awkward, my concern is usually trying not to make you feel awkward. You react to what I have to tell you in the way that naturally comes to you, but whilst you process this information for the love of God can you carry these drinks!

I used to love playing **pool** and having drinks with friends. What a combo! (By the way, if you want to take me on a date – make it a pub with a pool table…) However, I need to feel comfortable before I pick up that cue and chances are, I will now sit and watch you play instead.

Often my mates (the lads, wayyyyyy Stu and Luke!) will do teams so I can play but without the pressure of it being 1 against 1. Chances are that the team I am on will be the losing team, also if you see me holding a cue I would stay as far back as you can because who knows what will happen. I have wiped out a table of pint glasses before and decided I should probably not play anymore. I also can't break yet because I don't have enough strength in my arm yet, or I'll end up ruining the table. These are the little things that aren't a huge deal to you but are a massive thing to me.

Another thing is **relationships**. I am single, can you imagine dating...when they suggest going to a bar and it's time for me to get the drinks? I can't exactly just bring one back at a time, I would look mental (shut up) ...so if you are reading this and want to take me on a date, can we sit at the bar please? Thanks. It is a very difficult thing to talk about, not because

I want to hide it from people but because how do you start that as a conversation? I know you probably assume or think it isn't a big deal, but when you have to deal with these things on your own or have people in your little bubble help you open a jar, it really is a scary thing to open up and explain all of these things to someone new, so in the end I will admit I just don't bother.
I know, after all of this I'm trying to help you guys and tell you to let people help you and to tell others how you are feeling or about any issues you have...and then I'm here basically saying I'm scared of meeting someone, so I don't bother. That is taking the easy way out and it is something I have been working on, who knows maybe one day I'll fall in love with someone who likes me and my lucky fin, haha. What I am saying is that I feel it's a massive deal, and maybe it is to me but to someone else I guess it more than likely isn't right? If it is, I guess it's also their problem and not mine.
It is who I am and I'm just saying it will probably take me a long time to cut food that is on my plate if we go out for a meal, and I might do things that look awkward and different because it is what I have to do now.
Then again you might not even think twice or notice, and I have completely **overthought** the entire situation.

The kitchen is one of the main places I had to be assessed once I was home because of the safety of myself. Making a cup of tea needs to be done entirely with my left hand, because I once poured boiling hot water onto my left hand when I tried using my right. My wrist isn't strong enough to hold a kettle and pour it. My brain was still in the early stages of recovery and therefore my reaction to this was non-existent and I was left very burnt. Whilst I try my best to use my lucky fin as much as I can, there are circumstances in which it just isn't safe to do so. I cut myself a lot whilst chopping vegetables, I've even peeled my right hand with the peeler and my brain didn't register this nor did I feel pain until I saw the blood dripping all over the carrots. I love cooking and I love being able to cook for others, I do find it **overwhelming,** and a lot of thought needs to be involved so I tend to not want anyone in the kitchen when I am preparing food as I have to really concentrate. Also, if I am in a new kitchen, chances are I need to spend some time to **adapt** and work out how to hold the knife, and the safest hand to chop with. All these things in a normal day wouldn't cross your mind if you are able to use both of your hands, but when movement is limited in one limb it is really a lot to process daily.

I have two **adaptive** knives that I use, it's kind of like a saw, I guess. They are also as sharp as a saw too, and I have sliced myself a few times. With these adaptive knives it means I can use my lucky fin to chop food comfortably, I still need to focus as my brain is often slow to tell my left hand to move out of the way as all its focus is on my right hand.

Carrying trays in and out of the oven is sometimes difficult, again yes, I have burnt myself a lot. I often struggle because I want to be able to do these daily tasks, but often I need to **accept help** because it is just too heavy for my left hand to take all the strain. I have dropped so many of my meals due to not accepting help and it really can be frustrating not being able to do something that is just so easy for others and was once easy for me, something I took for granted before the stroke.

Driving is something I am SO glad that I am able to do. Before I was diagnosed with cancer, I was just about ready to book my test but then became too ill to, it was the last thing on my mind. After the stroke, when I was unable to walk or move my arms it became evident that I might not be able to drive again, or look after myself fully. A few years passed and recovery improved massively. I went to an assessment centre and drove for the first time in a very long while. At this point my right hand was able to grip and had more movement than before, however it was decided that I would drive an **automatic** as it would not have been safe to rely on my right hand to keep control whilst the left hand changed gear. Over time this has massively improved, and driving is one of those rare moments where my brain deems my body to be completely normal and I forget I have a weakness in my right arm at all. I do need to turn the key with my left hand but to be able to drive myself around in a car is a huge deal, especially when I was told I would **never walk again**.

Being able to drive myself around when I had to be looked after for so long, the **independence** of this is amazing. I appreciate my car so much; he is called Heisenberg. Whilst most people probably have a first car that is brand new, I just wanted anything that ran. I do not care that it is an old car, what I care about is the fact I am even able to drive one at all. It really makes you appreciate these things in life when everything was once taken away from you that the **material things** don't matter twice as much.

Shaking hands is something that I try to avoid, you know usually when people meet for the first time or if you have an interview you tend to shake the other person's hand? Well, I tend to awkwardly say "I'm a hugger, I don't do handshakes" which isn't something I would recommend at an interview, I'm yet to try that.

The reason being is because my brain tells my hand what to do...but delayed, by the time the other person's hand has reached mine they are either shaking my fist because my brain hasn't told my hand what the hell to do quick enough...or they shake my hand, with my thumb within their grip and 99% of the time I am unable to let go. I sometimes try and make a laugh out of it, but the reality is I have an awful handshake and there's no explaining why in these situations because it is just awkward and I hate making people feel uncomfortable, even though I'm the one that can't let go of your hand. I will let go eventually, but my brain is in shock and often I'll need to use my left hand to release the lucky fin's grip. I do also love hugs, so these are preferred.

HIGH FIVES. MAN, I MISS HIGH FIVES. I miss them. Now I'm not being rude if you have ever come at me for a high five and I've left you hanging. It is more than likely because you have naturally come towards my right hand...I now give the sloppiest high fives ever with my lucky fin or end up weakly punching the palm of your hand.
The other issue is if you go to my left hand, it's the same issue...sometimes it's a banging high five...but that's a yearly occasion, or I'll end up remarkably slapping myself in the face.

Catching & throwing. Yup, if someone throws something at me, chances are I won't react fast enough if it is veering towards the right side of my body, it'll probably smack me in the face. On the throwing side of things, it'll probably end up nearer to me than you...or again I'll probably somehow manage to throw it at myself.

Writing, typing, nail care, hairstyles, earrings, putting on a bra...these are some of the little things that again I am unable to do as I would have before the stroke. Okay so the latter isn't something that I get someone else to do, but if you wear a bra...are you able to put it on **one handed**? It is something that over time I have learnt to manage but as someone who wears a bra and would easily put this on in a few moments, it is something I struggled with massively at the start, but even now it is something that takes longer than normal as I have to adapt the way in which I do it.

Writing is now done with my left hand. There are times I'll practice with my lucky fin, but my brain is unaware of how to hold a pen in that hand. I came across an old diary of mine recently. I miss my writing, nowadays it's pretty unreadable unless I really concentrate and write slowly.

Typing is often done with my left hand only, depending on the keyboard sometimes I am able to use both hands to type but that is very rare.
As I am unable to hold and apply pressure onto a nail cutter, I go to get **manicures** done. Of course, I can use my left hand, but I cannot cut my left fingernails with my left hand. People often used to say I got this done a lot, but it is within reason, and it is a nice treat too so added bonus! **Hair**! It can take me AGES to tie my hair up in a ponytail or do anything with it which is often why I don't style it because it is tiring. It took me a long time to use both hands to be able to tie my hair in a ponytail, but even this can take up to 20 minutes still. **Earrings** are SO hard to put in **one handed**, I LOVE stud earrings, but I cannot put on the butterfly back, so this is something I have to get someone else to do, which is often my Mum. This is one thing I find very frustrating as it is a simple task that I just simply cannot do, so yes, I may need to ask for your help here, many times. That said, after two hours I've managed to get them in before…but that was only one side.

Mirror Box Therapy is something I love and something I have been using a lot more recently. How this works is that you put your affected limb into the box, out of sight. In my case it is my right hand. Then you place your good limb in view of the mirror. This tricks your brain into thinking that the reflection is your affected limb and looks as if you are moving it. I find this rewarding but also emotional. As when I look at the reflection it really is like I have my right arm back. Often it can get too much for me to do this exercise and I have learnt my limits, so I tend to only do these exercises a short amount of time before resting. I'll often do it before drumming so my arm is ready for what's to come.

Drumming is something I loved and love. I learnt to drum when I was about 15 and I used to drum for 4 hours every Sunday, play gigs in the week, and just generally drum all the time when I could. I'm not saying that I was incredible or anything but to go from playing how I used to be able to, to now only managing four minutes is a lot to deal with. I recently set my drums back up in the past few months. I have gone from 5 minutes drumming, to now being able to play for twenty minutes. Whilst this may not seem like an **achievement** to you, believe me when your brain told you for SO long that you only had a left arm and that right arm hanging off your body isn't your own limb, I am incredibly **proud** that I can even hold a drum stick again. It can get **frustrating** so again, I need to know my limits and to stop before I hit a bad place and the good emotions turn into bad ones. It's an incredible feeling where like driving, my brain deems it to be normal. The only difference is the right side of my body cannot keep up with the left and so it is incredibly challenging, but what's life without a challenge? Now if you ever ask me to drum for you the chances are, I'll get upset and annoyed at you and more than likely say no. This is because my brain knows how I used to be able to play, but my body no longer allows me to…not yet anyway. I am hopeful that I will be able to improve the more I keep at it, it just takes time.

Swimming is something that I was able to do before the stroke, I wasn't a strong swimmer but since the stroke I now have a huge **fear** of water. Me, my Mum, and sister Vicky all did adult swimming lessons a short while ago. This helped my confidence massively; it is still something that I am fearful of. So, whilst I want to be that person that jumps into the sea and have a great time, chances are I might not resurface. So, if you are having a laugh with me and push me off a boat on a holiday, it may be funny to you, but chances are when I'm splashing about screaming for you to save me - I am not joking, **please don't let me drown**. I do love the sea and the pool; I can swim but not for very long so I'll need to be somewhere I can have a quick escape if I need it. Also due to the weakness in my arm I won't be able to pull myself out, so please help me and don't make my fear any worse. Thanks in advance.

You do not know how lucky you are if you have never had a brain injury, or perhaps don't appreciate the fact that you don't actively have to think about doing something before doing it. Of course, I'm not saying it's a bad thing if you haven't had a brain injury, I do not wish it upon anyone.
What I am saying is that I never fully appreciated what I had before the stroke, before losing a massive part of me. So, the next time you butter your toast, just think of me who will more than likely have buttered her own hand and missed the toast entirely. When you turn on that light switch, just realise how quickly you do that small and simple task without even having to think about doing it.
You and your brain work together that you more than likely aren't even aware your brain just told you to read this, or that you dropped a pen, and your brain told you to pick it up. You just read this, and you just pick up the pen, right? For me I could stare at a pen for ages before my brain realises, I need one of my hands to pick it up. The trouble is where it still needs reminding, often these small tasks take a longer time. Appreciate every little thing that you are able to do because we shouldn't take them for granted.
I will admit there is probably a ton of things to this day that I am unable to do or HAVE to do with my left hand. There are so many things that I could mention here, so many little things that you guys are hopefully lucky enough that you are able to just do them, without thinking.
If you are like me and have to constantly think, and tell your brain something I am here with you and I completely get it – it is hard work, right? That brain of yours is incredible, and if

we need help...I guess we need to learn to ask for it, but that is hard. Hard because we have worked so long to be independent, yet those small things we still can't quite do are a massive deal and I guess we can't always do everything by ourselves. Even those of you reading this with a perfectly normal brain, unaffected by a stroke often need help. So, if I turn up at your house to open a jar for me it's probably because I am an hour in, and still can't open it and really want peanut butter.

I guess what I wanted to share with you all is that after a stroke life doesn't just return to normal. For many of us we are left with a lucky fin, or worse. For me I have been unsure as to sharing this with you all, especially as I have spent years trying to pass off as being "normal" to your eyes and to not have sympathy or be given that look.

However, I have learnt that it is a huge deal and at times I will avoid your help because I liked knowing that you didn't even notice. I love how unnoticeable the effect of the stroke has on me to you; but often I need you to notice. It is great that is unnoticeable to you because to me it is something I notice, live with, and have to be aware of otherwise I will walk into a wall again, or I will cut my hand and not the carrot.

Often, I'll need you to carry one of the bags, carry that tray or come with me to the bar. Often, I won't accept your help and I'll struggle even though I need your help. If I don't ask, then I won't get it. If you notice that I need your help, often it will upset me but only because my brain is in overdrive, and I am exhausted carrying those two cups of tea.

The next round is on me, but you guys are carrying your own drinks.

CHAPTER 20

THANK YOU

These two simple words can never be said enough after going through what I went through in 2006. Although it didn't begin and end in 2006, there were still battles I had to face for years to come. I cannot thank each of you enough.

There will never be enough words in existence to thank each of you. I may never have even had a chance to say these two words to you, but it meant the world having you by my side during the worst time of my life, so thank you.

Although I am thanking you guys, you of course wouldn't have been any other way. You were there for me, without me even asking you to be. You were there for me during my chemotherapy and when I shut off to most of you because I didn't know I had just woken up in ICU after suffering from a stroke. Though it was uncertain if I would survive this, most of you outside of my family and BFATT were none the wiser. Yet through not knowing what was going on you were still there when I eventually became stronger, though I was not myself or the 'Leena' you guys knew. This new version of me was accepted and we adapted to the new me, everyone adapted and adjusted before I did. Without you all I would

have struggled to get through each day.
If I haven't personally mentioned you, don't be disheartened, it is not my intention to appear as though I have forgotten you. There were so many of you caring, beautiful souls that visited me when I was probably dosed up on Chemo and in and out of naps, but it doesn't mean I don't appreciate you.

Mum and Dad

You were both there when the on-call doctor came over late that night to tell us that I urgently needed to go to the Bristol Haematology and Oncology centre. You both had a look in your eyes that I'll never forget, it is as if you knew before we were even told. As retired NHS nurses I guess you both knew what this particular hospital entailed.
When we were told that I had been diagnosed with Acute Myeloid Leukaemia you both were so strong and the best support I could ever ask for. To hear those words "You have Cancer" will never be forgotten, but I will also never forget you both squeezing my hand tightly whilst I cried when the doctors and nurses spoke to us until 4am. You are both the most amazing parents. Your love and care are second to none. You always put us first before yourselves.

Thank you for never leaving my side, for all your sleepless nights, for adapting the house so I was able to drag myself up the stairs before I was able to walk up them. Thank you for being patient with me when I was a moody teenager, and yes for still being patient with me if I get in a strop today, thank you.

Mum, thank you for cleaning my sick off me every other day, for having to bathe me when I was too weak or unable to. Thank you for cooking my favourite dishes for me and bringing them into the hospital for those days where I was able to eat.

Dad, thank you for carrying me, or physically holding me up when my legs were paralysed after the stroke. Thank you for always being at my side with mum. Thank you for watching every football game with me to distract me from what was really going on.

Thank you both for feeding me when I was unable to feed myself, for staying hopeful for me when I had given up. Neither of you ever gave up on me, you were both so strong and I don't think you even realised this at the time.
Thank you both for your unconditional love and getting me through the stroke even when you were told I would not survive, thank you for never giving up on me and helping me live.

I love you both and I thank both of you for everything then and thank you for everything now.

I love you Mum and Dad, thank you.

To the best siblings ever! **Vicky, Angel**, and **Ricki**.

You guys suck...

Haha kidding. I love you guys, of course I do. Even when you flick me in the face (Angel), or pour ketchup on my head (Ricki), or eat the last prawn from Mum's Pancit (Vicky.)

Angel
Thank you for keeping me company during my chemo and travelling to Bristol when you could during my treatments and numerous check-ups. Thank you for cleaning me up in the ICU numerous times which makes me gag and I can only imagine how gross that must have been for you, but you didn't even give it a second thought. Thank you for bringing in the PSP to try and keep my mind occupied away from what was going on. Thank you for quitting your job just so you could be near me when things got tough. Thank you for always providing me with nutritious recipes and kicking my health back into gear when all I wanted to do was eat pizza

every day. I'm having pizza tonight though, and no you can't stop me. Thank you for being strong for Mum, Dad and everyone else, and holding things together for the family. Thank you for the holidays we have been on when I thought the ICU ward would be the last thing I ever saw. Thank you for not only cooking me amazing meals but for taking me to the most incredible restaurants like you promised you would when I was dying in the ICU. Thank you for being the best big sister ever...even if I am SLIGHTLY taller than you. Yoda.

Vicky
Thank you for staying by my side in hospital and bringing me yummy snacks when I was able to eat in between my chemo. Thank you for reading those trashy magazines to me in ICU with Angel and making me smile and laugh even though I wasn't physically able to show these emotions yet. Thank you for going on those 530am runs with me when I was able to not only walk but run again. Thank you for doing the Race For Life with me whilst Ali was alive to raise awareness, and then again when she had passed away. Thank you for working for CLIC Sargent when you did, because you contributed to one of the best charities, and one that helped me when I needed them. Thank you for coming to visit me when I was away with CLIC Sargent for the Hot House music workshop that they ran so that I was able to enjoy it with you and share my love of Sam Brookes with you too. Thank you for bringing Luke in to see me, even when he was just 7 years old just so I was able to see my nephew and his cheeky face. **Luke** thank you for coming to see me and for waving at me from the corridor. I know it must have been scary to see me like that, but you made my day. I remember that day and moment vividly, and I remember it being a bad one until I saw you. So, thanks dude; now go clean some dishes in between playing your games before your Mum gets annoyed at you, okay?

Ricki
Big broooo! Bogeyyyyyy!!!! Thank you. Thank you for all your visits when I was unwell and for winding me up like you usually do (in a good way, like how a big bro would wind up a little sister and get away with it because he's the only boy. MUMMM, DADDDD, he's picking on me again). Thank you for always looking out for me and for making me laugh when things weren't looking too great. Thank you for always making sure I was doing my hand exercises after the stroke when I was struggling with them. Thank you for telling me I looked nice and suited a bald head; thank you for laughing with me when I used to refer to myself as Howard. Thank you for telling me to ignore others when I feared what people might think about how I looked. Thank you for going through with that blood test with our sisters to see if any of you were a match to me, in case I needed anything further down the line. I knew you hated needles, but not that much. Thank you for basically passing out for me, and no I won't apologise for laughing at you as I had three needles going into my body at the time, haha love ya bro.
Thanks for one of the greatest presents of all, Wispa. Thank you for bringing this most adorable, cheeky, hilarious, and sweet puppy into our home.

Thanks to all of you awesome sibs for being there not only for me, but for each other; including Mum and Dad. Thanks to each of you awesome siblings for being you. You guys are the best.

Thanks to my sister-in-law **Carly** and to my brother-in-law **Lee** for being incredible. Though you weren't part of our family whilst I was ill back in 2006, you're there if I ever need my food chopped up, or more importantly you're there when my wine glass is running low haha.

Wispa

Thank you for your unconditional love and for making us all smile. I have always loved dogs and had always wanted one for as long as I can remember.

When I was in ICU Mum and Dad promised I could have one, on one condition; I needed to survive.

That slight glimmer of hope, of thinking I need to survive not only because I am not yet done in the world, I was only 18, it wasn't my time...but also, I need to be alive to look after a dog if I get one!

WISPA!!

The absolute beauty of a Labrador, I don't care if any of you are judging me right now about thanking a dog, because he was the biggest part of my recovery and a massive part of our family, so if you don't like it, tough that's not my problem. He was the most incredible dog, so smart, so happy to see you always. He always knew if you or if anyone else was sad and would follow you around and comfort you and lick away

your tears. He would open the door for me if I was carrying things and then run away with Dad's socks because he knew I couldn't chase him whilst carrying stuff. He helped my recovery because he must have sensed I had a weak arm. He would always go to my right side of my body to encourage me to stroke him with my lucky fin. My brother brought him home one day, and Mum wasn't really a fan of big dogs so we both kind of told her he was fully grown when he hit 6 months...Haha, sorry Mum but aren't you glad we had him?
He helped my recovery after going through cancer and a stroke, he got me out of the house and helped build up my confidence and independence.

We sadly had to say goodbye to him in 2019 because cancer took him, yup my cancer dog was taken away by cancer! I hope he and Ali are somewhere having fun together eating cucumbers and carrots, because those were his fave.
Actually, he ate everything, he wasn't fussy...even foxes' poo occasionally for a cheeky snack mid walk, gross.

Rest in Peace my lil buddy, thank you for the best 11 years of unconditional love that you brought into our lives.

The Besties.

To all of my amazing friends, to which I am grateful for but there are too many to mention, and I'd need another 20 chapters but **Sandee, Izzy & Soph.** You guys. Thank you for everything, for always being there no matter what and for picking me up constantly when I was down. Thank you for coming with me to the never-ending check-ups, or for being there afterwards.

Thank you for everything you did, and for EVERYTHING you do. I will never forget it; I am so lucky to have friends like you in my life. Each of you are the most incredible people, strong, determined, and caring. All of you are the most incredible friends that I could have ever asked for and especially during that time. I would joke about drumming with "carrot sticks" when I was waking up from a general anaesthetic. We all gagged at the tomato soup which had a layer of skin, safe to say I did not eat that. Each of your visits made a massive difference even if just seeing you leave after waking up. I would wake up to little notes or presents to say that you had been. Your constant care and friendship are something I will cherish forever. I love you guys and will never be able to thank you enough.

Becky

My favourite emo pal. Through all my treatment you were there for me, it is not forgotten. We may have lost contact during that time, but I am so pleased we managed to reconnect, and I am so excited that you are back in my life. Words really can't express that enough. My life wasn't the same without you in it, I cannot wait for all the emo gigs we can finally go to again.

Clare

Lil Clare. Thank you for sneaking me in Pic 'n Mix when I wasn't allowed it, it was the most glorious thing ever, even if I did feel a little sick afterwards; it was totally worth it! Thank you for always being there for me. I'm looking forward to the Ibiza sun again and our little trips to gigs abroad. Gym buddy for life.

BFATT thank you, especially to you and your family and all your friends, thank you. It was a tough journey to say the least, but I couldn't have done it without you by my side. BFATT thank you for everything. Thank you for driving home 6hrs that one time from Scotland so you could come to an appointment with me, but passing out before I had to leave as you were so tired from the journey. Thank you for everything that you did, and for being there for me, and for your families love and care throughout. I wish you all the best in life and all the happiness. To his friends - thank you, you guys are awesome, and I loved each of you.

St Brendan's Sixth Form College to ALL of you from St Brendans Sixth Form in 2006. Andy Morgan, Dan, Donna, Charlie, Josh (from the band The Hit Ups), for the incredible card you made Josh... I loved it; signed by all my friends at college - thank you. To the 30 of you who all came at the same time during a visit to me and the doctor laughing saying he had never seen a patient with so many visitors during his entire career but especially on one day. Thank you for making me that patient, the visitors I had during this entire time helped me in ways you would never imagine, thank you.

Macmillan, though I think I passed out from chemo during one of your many visits – thank you. Your support to me and my family during such a hard time was amazing. Thank you for helping fund towards a laptop so that I could watch movies during my blood transfusions. Thank you for your help financially after I was discharged. This was a stressful time for me and my family, to be told that I shouldn't be getting certain benefits because "she's not that unwell" was hard to hear. Especially as I was unable to walk, talk and do anything myself for quite some time, your help in these cases helped more than you'll ever know; thank you.

CLIC Sargent thank you for inviting me to Glastonbury

Festival in 2008 and Beach Break Live Festival in 2010. Thank you, Phil Day.

Glasto thanks go to - Phil, Sally Archer, Kate Wheeler, Ali (including her incredible family and friends), Alex, Charlotte, Harry, Jess, Katie, Matt, Michael, Nikki and Ryan (RIP xx). Special thanks to all the bands and artists that took time to meet us or allowed us to watch from side stage Kate Nash, The Subways, The Editors, The Fratellis, Kings Of Leon, The Raconteurs, The Verve, Foals, Mark Ronson, Groove Armada, Patrick Watson, The Ting Tings, The Kills, The Cribs, Emmy The Great, Hilltop Hoods, Vampire Weekend, The Courteeners, The Futureheads, Biffy Clyro, The Rocketeers, Psycho Baby, The Stars & Spiritualised.

Clic Sargent music workshop thanks go to - Will Lang, Phil Day, Sam Brookes, Adam Newton, Sam Nadel, Claire, Simon Whitehead and Katie.

CLuMsY, Joel, Patch and Siggy – thank you for the most incredible memories during our Remix music workshop days before I fell ill. These will never be forgotten, playing the kazoo, random jamming sessions & the best fish finger sandwiches ever.

The Louisiana, Bristol. To the bands that held a fundraiser for me at The Louisiana on Saturday 19th August 2006 in Bristol whilst I was in hospital, thank you:
Gaslamp Quarter, Fallout Trust, Nova Saints, Los Conios, Figment, Blackbud, Fortune Drive, Amelia Tucker, Rob Sharples, cLuMsY, The Hats. Special thanks to Mig and his Dad for hosting this event at one of my favourite venues during my teenage years.

Jack, James & Dainty my Jazz Hop Café Fam! After taking the Foundation Degree in Photography I met Jack & James.

We lost contact for a short while, then reconnected. I now have the best job in the world, and working alongside your friends is one of the greatest feelings in the world.
We wind each other up, sometimes I can't handle the banter, sometimes I go too far with my banter, but it just works. Thanks, Jack, for giving me this chance to work with you and for all the incredible trips we've been able to do as part of it. Thank you, James, for always being caring and giving back the best banter. Thank you, Dainty, for dealing with us as I know we're pretty annoying (mainly me, I know guys) thanks for cooking us awesome food whilst we're working hard in the studio. Thanks to each of you for putting up with my annoying can-do positive attitude and being there whenever the hard times hit. Love you guys!

Yoann Garel thank you for being the soundtrack behind my book and one of the reasons that I finally completed it. You are one of the kindest people I have met through working at The Jazz Hop Café, and I can't say enough what a pleasure it has been to have met you and to hear your music. I wish you all the best with your career my friend.

Swevennnnnnn aka Luke thank you for being a shoulder to cry on and for always listening and being there for me when I've needed you. Thanks for putting up with my constant mood changes and for making sure my smile never drops for too long.

Thank you to the new friends I have made within the lofi scene, though I am not really able to play the drums anymore to hear each of you create incredible music that each hits the feels in a different way is really something special, the first thing I notice is a decent drum beat – no pressure haha.

Craig, Aimee, Holly, Josh, Ollie, Sam, Jess, James, Hana, Aidan and Steve. You are all a bunch of weirdos in the best way possible. Thanks for your friendships and for the laughs over the years, with many more to come. Rest in peace Steve, you absolute legend. We love you to the moon and back.

The Cuban Heels - Thank you **Dan** for always checking in on me and visiting me when I really craved Worcester Sauce crisps. Thank you for going to several shops to try and find some!

The Naturals. Felix, Harry, Kai & **Rob**. You guys were my favourites, such incredible kids and always made me laugh from the Remix days. Thank you for your visits, cards and for being the most caring and loveliest of people. I say kids but I don't think you guys are anymore, you are still the most caring and incredible bunch and I miss you lot!
ROB! ROBBB. Thank you for coming to visit me pretty much every day after school. For sitting at the end of my room on a chair, doing your homework whilst I dosed in and out. For reading to me, for making me laugh, for song writing or singing to me. You sir are an absolute blessing. You were like the younger brother I never had; this simple gesture made me feel lucky to know you. Thank you for making sure that when I woke up, I was never alone and for staying until other people arrived so that I was never alone too long. Thank you to your Mum for allowing you to visit so often when you probably should've been at home studying or hanging out with your friends. You were only 15 yet were the best friend ever. A little back story as to how I know Rob & their band 'The Naturals'. I used to do song writing sessions with my band Incured before I fell ill. This was called Remix and ran by local band cLuMsY. The Naturals were one of the bands that also went, and they are the cutest. Although they have all grown up now, I still picture them as the sweet 14/15-year-old kids that used to come and visit me and play songs to me when I was unable to play.

Incured
THANK YOU. Thank you for being a huge part of my life in my early teens, for letting me live the emo dream of being a drummer in this band.
Rosie, Steve & Mark I will cherish these memories forever. Thank you for coming in to see me and doing a little jam session in my room, I was told it made the entire ward smile so thank you for not only making my day, but for making theirs too. Steve and Rosie, thank you for arranging the charity event at the Louisiana. Special thanks to each of your families too, for driving you to the hospital to come and visit me. Especially to you, **Sally** (Rosie's mum). Thank you for always being there and for being a fun place to hang out with Rosie and the band in my teenage years & for always feeling like home.

Thanks for editing my book and for being a friend for life Rosie, forever living that emo dream. May we always laugh like this in life.

Thank you to each of you that I perhaps met after everything I had been through in 2006 up until this very moment, thank you. Thanks for carrying my drinks, opening jars for me, and carrying me through to the next day.

Thank you to everyone that sent me their wishes, cards, gifts and flowers.

Thanks to the **Beirne's family** for their continuous prayers at St Joseph's Church whilst I was ill. Your family have always supported us from day one and will never stop. We love you all. Special thanks to my Godmother Christine who in the very early stages of this book helped with the editing.

I mention these guys last but not least.
Thank you, **Doctor Roger Evely**, thank you for saving my life. Hearing the word 'Cancer' is tough, having you as my Oncologist was and will always be unforgettable.
Doctor Ray, thank you for being the only one that managed to do Bone Marrow Biopsies even when they hurt so much you always managed to get it done with the least amount of pain possible.
To every nurse from the NHS in the Bristol Haematology and Oncology Centre from May 2006 – April 2011. I can't remember all your names but that doesn't mean I have forgotten you. Sheryll, Rose and JP to name a few thank you. To each and every one of you for saving my life, holding my hand, for your care when I was too weak to care for myself, for holding my hair back whilst I threw up (when there was hair to be held), for taking a few moments on your way home just to say bye to me and telling me that you would see me in the morning.
Not only to the nurses in the Oncology centre but a thank you to EVERY single person that set foot in that building to care for me.

To the cleaners who cleaned my room from 5am every morning, but quietly as to not wake me or my Mum, Dad or BFATT or whoever's shift it was on the armchair. To not only be caring but to take the time to ask me how I was each day. Thank you.

To all the kitchen staff who would go out of their way to provide food for me when the side effects got so bad. To uncover the food outside of my room before bringing it in, so that the smell wasn't too overwhelming. Cutting the crusts off my sandwiches when I became too weak to chew. For not only feeding me but offering tea and coffee to my Mum and offering her food even though you probably weren't supposed to.

Thank you to the Frenchay Brain Injury Rehabilitation Unit (BIRU) team, December 2006 – February 2007. Thank you for getting my life back. Without you I wouldn't be able to type this, would be unable to speak, walk or run.

Thank you, **Doctor Holloway,** for assessing me and having me in BIRU, I do not know what I would be like now without the strong, dedicated and determination you and your team had.

Thank you to The Frenchay Head Injury Therapy Unit 2007 (HITU) thank you. Thank you for helping me live my life the most 'normal' way possible. For helping me further with exercises and helping me adapt to my new way.

Thank you to the intermediate care team – Daisy, thank you and your team for everything.

Thank you, **Sandee**, for editing my words when they were blog posts in lockdown and thank you **Rosie** for helping me bring those words on my blog to become the book that you are now reading.

Thank you, **Ben**, for bringing my book cover to life and to create what I had in my mind so perfectly. Thank you **Aleks** for taking this photograph, knew it'd come in handy one day! To every single person that helped in getting me where I am today and to those of you that still help me, I cannot thank you enough. If you aren't mentioned within my book, I apologise if that upsets you in any way, it is not my intention. If you were there during this time I cannot thank you enough, you'll know who you are it's not that I have forgotten you, but I think we may run out of paper if I continue.

Thank you for picking up my book and reading it.

To all the new friends I have made along the way, thank you for being in my life.

I am lucky to be alive.

Thank you for then, thank you for now.

AML is a very aggressive form of cancer, it can develop and spread rapidly which explains why I felt so lifeless before diagnosis. There is a very low survival rate to this type of cancer. I remember being on a ward with an elderly lady that was having treatment for this cancer, for the second time. This terrified me, I was only on my second course of chemo when I met her, and I was already scared.
However, here I am. We never know what tomorrow brings but we live for today. When you wake up each morning, make it the best day - treat it like your last. Tell the people close to you that you love them, that you're grateful for them because one day you might not be able to.

Enjoy the highs in life, the best moments and make them outweigh your bad days. Fill yourselves with positivity even if that is just getting up and out of bed, enjoy the little victories.

Life is a gamble, own it and win it.

ABOUT THE AUTHOR

Wait, what.
I'm an author now?
Well, that is wild.

To think how long ago I began writing this book to have now finally completed it, is crazy.
I'm Leena, if you hadn't already worked that out, this is my first book ever! If you're reading this, I'd love to hear from you. I'm just a hyper weirdo who tries her very best to stay positive and enjoy each day as best as possible.
I really hope you enjoyed my book; it has taken a very long time to complete but I set my mind to it, and it is now finally out in the world!

Printed in Great Britain
by Amazon

23097373R00126